THE RLH ALBUM
Peter Gascoine

RLH 13 (KYY 513) on layover at Amersham Station in 1956. Note the wheel scotch by the offside front wheel, a common practice then where terminals were on a steep slope.

Photo *Alan B.Cross/Allen Smith*

Contents

Introduction

It was in November 1950 when my first encounter was made with a London Transport RLH vehicle, this being on my school journey from Addlestone to Weybridge passing the Weymann coach builders factory during the journey. Standing at the bus stop in Church Road, Addlestone this gleaming new green double-decker pulled up and certainly impressed myself and other waiting passengers. From this day the RLH has remained the vehicle most admired by myself and this album is dedicated to the 76 vehicles in the class with an updated history for the 65 years between 1950 and 2015.

It is now nearly forty years since my first publication on the RLH, which was followed by a second 'The London RLH Remembered' in 1995, this Album summarises part of the text from the two previous publications with updates of the current known owners and locations of the majority of the 35 remaining vehicles.

Additional chapters are included detailing London's early Lowbridge buses plus a section on the Midland General RLHs.

This Album is hoped to portray the affection for the RLH which has seen 65 years since its introduction and now remains part of London's history.

Photo Right - The Author enjoys helping out on RLH 8 working route 461 between Walton and Staines.

Front Cover - RLH 62 (MXX 262) rounds the bends in Parkside Way, North Harrow en route for Rayners Lane on 11th June 1969, just a few days before the route was converted to the one-man-operated H1. **Photo** Mike Hodges

Acknowledgements

The production of the RLH Album would not have been possible without the assistance from the several dedicated persons to whom I am most grateful. Alan B.Cross for assistance with the early days of the London lowbridge buses plus photographs; Maurice Bateman for various research, mainly in the disposal section plus a selection of photographs; Chris Elkin for the Midland General section; Ken Glazier for part detail included in 'The RLH Story 1950-1971' and Andrew Gascoine for his design, layout and type setting.

Following the two former publications relating to the RLH, several comments and photographs received from readers have proved most useful in keeping and updating the history of the vehicles. This information is used within the album with a special thank you to Mrs Grace Rickard for various detail and photographs.

Photographs are credited individually with a selection also from the Author's collection, several of which were taken by unidentified photographers and therefore thanks are also passed to these persons.

First published in 2015 in Great Britain by; Modelstone Bus Club, 3 Ayrefield Grove, Shevington, Wigan, Lancashire WN6 8DZ

ISBN   978-0-9934361-0-9   Copyright July 2015 Peter Gascoine

British Library Cataloguing in Publication Data A catalogue record for this book is available from the British Library

Printed in Great Britain by South Ribble Printing Limited.

The Early days of the London 'Lowbridge' Buses

Following the formation of the London Passenger Transport Board in 1933 lowbridge double deck vehicles were introduced to Country Area route 336 (Chesham - Watford). Eight AEC Regents classified STs were obtained to pass under the Metropolitan Line's bridge at Amersham Common which had a height clearance of 13 ft 6 inches. 1934 saw a further Country Area route the 410 (Reigate - Bromley North Station) which passed under a low bridge at Oxted in Surrey being converted with twelve new AEC's based at Godstone garage.

On the 30th October 1940 the first recorded lowbridge bus to enter service in the Central Area was allocated to Sutton garage this being loaned Plymouth Corporation Dennis Lance DR9634.

For many years Sutton garage operated route 245 (Morden station - South Wimbledon station) via the low railway bridge at Worcester Park and had the real need to convert the single deck route to double deck.

Lowbridge ST 141 (GF7217) seen travelling along Watford High Street on the 9th July 1946 prior to final rebuilding.

Photo *Alan B.Cross*

On the 22nd January 1941 the route was re-numbered 127 and converted to lowbridge operation using provincial lowbridge buses on town work including several from the Manchester Corporation and Hants and Dorset fleets. With the departure of the provincial buses during August 1941 the Central Area no longer had any such vehicles available for the 127.

In August 1941 five of the Country Area ST's were repainted red, transferred to the Central Area and allocated to Sutton garage for route 127 making up half of the required allocation of 10, the remainder being provided by LT single-deckers. Operation of the route was transferred to Merton garage on 29th October 1941 along with the STs, the balance now being provided by Qs.

There was now an urgent need for more lowbridge buses in the Central Area as well as the Country Area. Over a ten month period between October 1942 and June 1943 Chiswick Works produced 20 lowbridge bodies which were mounted onto existing STL chassis. Initially five went to Merton garage to replace the STs, which were transferred back to the Country Area. The remainder went to Harrow Weald and Addlestone garages. The Harrow Weald route 230 had to negotiate two low bridges and the STLs replaced Qs which were unable to cope with the heavy loadings on that route.

Lowbridge STL 2720 (DYL 853) Working route 230 on the 29th October 1952.   **Photo** Alan B.Cross

Top Left - New "utility" Daimlers (D1-6) were delivered to Merton garage during April and May 1944 and a further four (D128 - 131) arrived in November 1945 releasing STLs for use elsewhere. Lowbridge Daimler D1 (GXE 578) pauses at New Malden 'Fountain' working route 127 during October 1948.
Photo Alan B. Cross

Top Right - STL 1046 (BPF 270) at Staines West Station.
Photo J.H.Aston

Lower Right - The Godstone STLs were sent to Addlestone including STL 1055 (BPF 458). Seen here leaving Walton-on-Thames on the 30th December 1952 working route 461A to Botleys Park Hospital.
Photo by the late C Carter

The new generation lowbridge RLH arrives with London Transport

KYY 510 (RLH 10), with body work built at Weymann's, Addlestone Surrey, delivered to London Transport then returning to the Surrey countryside for a photo shoot before entering service during June 1950 at Addlestone garage - just 800 yards from Weymanns.

THE RLH STORY 1950-1971

WHILST IN PASSENGER SERVICE WITH LONDON TRANSPORT AND LONDON COUNTRY

Following the need to replace the ageing and mixed lowbridge fleet of vehicles in 1950 London Transport was given the opportunity to obtain twenty AEC Regent IIIs with lowbridge bodies, built to a standard pattern by Weymann's of Addlestone and originally intended for the Midland General Company. This batch of vehicles were purchased and formed the 'RLH' (Regent Low Height) class.

RLH 72 (MXX 272) stands between RT 4435 (NXP 789) and RT 855 (JXN 233) at Morden Station terminus.

Photo Alan B.Cross

The Chassis were model 9612E and like the RT, of which this was the provincial version having the AEC 9.6 litre engine derated to 115 bhp, fluid flywheel and air operated pre-selective gearbox. They differed from the RT in having a high bonnet line, giving a longer chrome plated radiator and an engine-driven dynamo together with the top engine air cleaner (which gave rise to the bulge in the bonnet side). The performance of these vehicles was very similar to the RT but the characteristic thump of the deeper engine note clearly distinguished them.

The vehicles were completed and all delivered to London Transport in Country Area green livery; classified 1 RLH1 numbered RLH1-20 with registrations KYY 501-520. The first six entering service from Amersham garage in May and June 1950 on route 336 with the remainder of the batch being allocated to Addlestone (7-14) and Godstone (15-20) and entering service by July 1950.

All the STLs at Addlestone were sent to Godstone and together with the RLHs 15-20 dislodged the forward entrance STLs from their home garage for the last time. On 27th September 1950 the group of single deck services running south from Woking were converted to lowbridge double deck operation.

The September 1950 route changes in the South West area gave Addlestone a total requirement of 18 lowbridge vehicles an increase of 12 and several Godstone STLs were returned to service to augment the RLHs. Guildford now joined the ranks of garages operating lowbridge buses and received 6 STLs.

On July 11th 1952 because of the closure of Leavesden Road Garage, route 336 was diverted in Watford from Pond Cross Roads via the High Street to Watford High Street Garage. Later that year on October 19th the Sunday afternoon and evening service on route 463 was diverted at Send over the 436A to Ripley, leaving only an hourly service via Merrow to Guildford. The 436A journeys were curtailed at Woking and became part of the 436.

Towards the end of 1952 the first of a repeat order for 56 RLHs joined the London Transport fleet. These were model 9613E Regents and were virtually identical to the first batch, the most obvious differences being their polished aluminium radiators, lack of roof vents, front cab drivers vent and used ticket box on the platform now the standard black hinged box. RLH 21-76 were classified 2RLH1/1 and received the registrations MXX 221-276, the first 32 being green and the remainder red. All had been delivered by January 1953.

A rare occasion was RLH 56 (MXX 256) meeting trolleybus 1560 (FXH 560) at Aldgate.
Photo *Alan B.Cross*

The first two RLHs 21 & 22 went to Godstone releasing two STLs which went to Harrow Weald to replace the two STs but before the 410 was completed, seven were sent to Addlestone and eight to Guildford to replace the STs and STLs. Route 415 (Guildford-Ripley) previously operated by RTs now shared the Guildford allocation of RLHs with the 436 group, although there was no physical need for low bridge operation. East Grinstead received four RLHs for route 424 (Reigate-East Grinstead) and 428 (East Grinstead - Dormansland) replacing RTs and highbridge STLs.

The remaining five green vehicles were allocated to Amersham garage to work routes 305/A (Beaconsfield/Chelfont Common-Gerrards Cross) and 359 (Aylesbury-Amersham) again replacing STLs and RTs. This allocation of lowbridge vehicles to routes on which they were not essential gave the Country Bus department for the first time a number of spare buses and the days of vehicle shortage were at last brought to an end. The 24 red vehicles were allocated to Harrow Weald (14) and Merton (10) the later receiving its first in advance of the main batch and before the 230 allocation was complete. So the London lowbridge fleet reached its peak, with a total of 76 vehicles and operated on a larger number of routes then ever before.

Red RLH 57 (MXX 257) meets green RLH 37 (MXX 237) in Station Road, Redhill.
Photo Alan B.Cross

Above - RLH 7 (KYY 507) repainted in Central Area red livery working route 178.

Left - RLH 51 (MXX 251) at Ripley Post Office terminus of route 415.

Routes 436 and 436A were diverted between Woodham and Woking Station to serve the new Sheerwater LCC Estate from August 5th 1953 leaving the unchanged 463 to deal with the traffic on the old route. On the 6th October 1954 some weekday journeys on route 415 were extended via Portsmouth Road and Ockham Lane to the village of Ockham about two and half miles east of Ripley. On the same date one RLH was sent to Reigate to operate the heavily used weekday short workings between Redhill and the estate at Mersham on route 447. Low bridges in Battlebridge Lane had precluded the use of any kind of double decker previously but the introduction of traffic light controlled single line working under the brick arch now rendered it safe for low bridge vehicles.

On March 16th 1955 the single deck vehicles on Central Bus route 248 (Upminster, Hall Lane-Cranham) which served a rapidly developing new estate and passed under a low bridge in St.Mary's Lane was replaced by 3 RLHs. The vehicles were obtained from the routes 424 and 428 which received RTs instead. The spare RLH was often found working route 249 (Corbets Tay-Upminster Station) which was then London Transports shortest route.

Two Country Area green vehicles were transferred to the Central Area for use on routes 248/9. Vehicles involved were RLH 22 and 23 which were eventually painted red for the purpose. From May 1955 Staines garage occasionally borrowed RLHs from Addlestone at weekends to work duplicate journeys on Green Line route 725 (Windsor-West Croydon) which passed under Worcester Park Bridge.

The seven week strike in the summer of 1958 saw a reduction in the requirements for the RLH. Central Area route 127 was withdrawn after the 19th August and various other amendments were made to both Central and Country Area routes reducing the overall Monday-Friday schedule requirement from 67 to 53 (16 Central and 37 Country).

The surplus of RLHs which the cuts had thrown up enabled the Executive to introduce double-deckers on to the high frequency single deck route 208A (Clapton Pond - Maryland Station) which boasted a number of low bridges. Some of these were too low even for RLHs and the route had to be diverted from Homerton High Street via Marsh Hill, Homerton Road, Lee Conservancy Road, Eastway, Wick Road, Chapman Road and White Hart Lane to Carpenters Road in which form it no longer bore much relation to the 208 and was accordingly renumbered 178. The new service which required 15 RLHs for a peak vehicle requirement of 13 allocated to Dalston garage was introduced on May 13th 1959. The RLHs allocated to Dalston were augmented by four ex Country buses (7, 29, 49 and 52) which were repainted red and brought the schedule requirement back to 67 vehicles.

The winter timetable of 1959 which started on October 14th brought another recruit to the lowbridge buses, when one RLH was allocated to Addlestone garage for use on Monday - Friday route 420 (West Byfleet to Woking Station via Sheerwater Estate).

From August 2nd 1964 the Sunday schedule on routes 461 and 461A which had not had to pass under any low bridges for eight years was withdrawn from the 436 and 463 schedule and hence forth was operated by RTs.

Because of the enforced use of different types of vehicle the schedules for the 410 and 411 were both inefficient involving long layovers at Reigate. Apart from any desire to standardise its fleet, London Transport had long been anxious to convert the 410 to highbridge operation to enable joint compilation of its timetable with route 411 to eliminate this inefficiency. Consequently, on November 4th 1964 the 410 was diverted via East Hill Road, East Hill, Snatts Hill, Station Road East, Gresham Road and Grandville Road, a tortuous and roundabout route in Oxted to avoid the low bridge. RTs took over from the RLHs on the same day. This date saw the decline commence for the RLH class.

Routes 436A and 461 were withdrawn altogether on Sundays from November 1st 1964 and the 461 ran for the last time on a Saturday on December 24th 1966.

On October 31st 1965 route 336 was converted to one man operation using RFs. As the 461A had been converted to RT operation earlier the same year on June 30th the total number of RLHs now scheduled in the Country Area on Monday's to Friday's was a mere 16.

RLH 15 (KYY 515) Seen on a short working of route 410 to Biggin Hill (Black Horse).

Photo *J.H.Aston*

In the Central Area there had been less changes, although the number of RLHs scheduled had slowly declined, paticularly at weekends. On October the 16th 1962 a new route, normally RT operated and numbered 230A was introduced between Harrow Weald Garage and Northwick Park Station to serve Kenton Lane. It did not pass under any lowbridges but authority was given for the use of RLHs when necessary, in practice this seems to have been the normal allocation.

The Monday to Friday off-peak and Saturday service lasted only until August 16th 1963 and the route was finally withdrawn altogether after January 21st 1966 when it was replaced by an extension of route 209 (South Harrow-Harrow Weald). Meanwhile, over in Essex the 248 had lost its Sunday service after November 15th 1964.

RLH 73 (MXX 273) Passes under the 13'-9" bridge at Cranham on 19th April 1964.

Photo *Geoff Mills*

June 1965 saw the only livery change which involved all Central Area vehicles receiving flake grey relief bands in place of the cream used previously upon repaint. Country Area vehicles were not effected.

The decline in the Country Area continued with route 447 losing its RLH allocation after 24 December 1967 leaving only Addlestone and Guildford garages operating the RLH in the Country Area, plus three garages in the Central Area using a maximum of 38 vehicles on Monday to Friday workings.

The next drastic reduction was in the Central Area when route 230 was converted to MBS operation on 14 June 1969.

With the formation of London Country Bus Services on 1 January 1970, 17 Country Area RLHs were transferred to this operator - these being: RLHs 13, 14, 21, 24, 25, 26, 31, 32, 33, 34, 35, 36, 44, 45, 46, 47 and 50. Legal lettering was changed to read Bell Street, Reigate, Surrey and the fleet name panels were painted out together sadly with the triangle badge on the radiator. London Country fleet names were applied gradually but no other livery change took place.

The RLHs had only a very short life with their new owner, and during the Spring of 1970 both Addlestone and Guildford garages would be losing their RLH allocations. After just twenty years and one month RLH 14 had a record that no other RLH could claim. It left the body builders at Addlestone in June 1950, was allocated to Addlestone garage for its complete working life, passing Weymanns possible 16 times a day until being withdrawn on 31st July 1970.

Photo RLH 31 (MXX 231) arrives at Addlestone Garage on 31st July 1970 for the final time, being fuelled and prepared for transfer to Garston Garage for storage.

The 31st July 1970 saw the majority of RLHs being taken off service early evening to be ferried to Garston garage for storage. RLH 35 which had been allocated running number WY13 was to complete its duty arriving at Woking Station from Guildford at 22.41 where driver Todman and conductor Mc-Leod took over for the final run. The bus was not particularly crowded during the journey but by the time it reached Addlestone there were streamers everywhere. RLH 35 arrived at Addlestone garage at 23.09 where it was quickly stripped of destination blinds and prepared for a ferryman to take it to Garston garage where it needed to arrive before midnight.

Although this was officially the last journey for a Country RLH it was not so in practice!! RLH 44 working GF 16 was changed for an RF during the evening however this got changed back by the crew operating the last workings and therefore several of the late journeys on route 461A were operated by this vehicle between Ottershaw and Walton finally arriving at Addlestone garage at 23.17 from Walton just eight minutes after the official last journey. This vehicle being late on arrival remained stored at Addlestone garage pending its conversion into a mobile uniform stores for London Country Bus Services.

Photos *Nearing the end of their life with London Country on the 18th July 1970 RLH 14 (KYY 514) is seen passing under the low bridge departing from Staines and RLH 34 (MXX 234) is seen also on Route 436A at Chertsey Lane.*

The remaining London Transport Central Area RLHs were then set for withdrawal; routes 248/A being converted to SMS operation from 18 September 1970. This left just one route, the 178 which was the last Central Area route to commence RLH operation on 13 May 1959 and now the last to operate them. The date was announced as 16 April 1971 and RLH 61 duly emerged as D3 for the evening peak service on that day. Unlike the Country Area route 178 operated the full service for the day with RLHs and on the last journey of all from Stratford to Clapton Pond at 20.35, RLH 61 was fully laden for this ceremonial journey. Leaving Clapton Pond on time RLH 61 entered Dalston garage a few minutes late at 21.17 after which is was reprieved for a further day when on the 17 April it operated a private hire covering former RLH territory both in the Country and Central Area. It was then stored at Poplar for a few days before being exported to Canada.

Shortly before the demise of the RLH on Central Area route 178 the following statement was given in the London Transport publicity leaflet

'Unfortunately the only buses which London Transport operate which are able to pass under the low railway bridges in Carpenters Road are single deckers which are too long and too wide to negotiate some of the roads served by bus route 178'

The RLH was now only a memory to the travelling public of the London suburbs, but with a large number of the vehicles being re-sold for further use their story up to the year 1971 is far from complete....

RLH 61 (MXX 261) which was the final one in service and although exported to Canada has now returned to the UK being amongst Ensigns Heritage Fleet, seen arriving at Victoria Station on 28th October 2005. **Photo** *Alan Conway*

The London Transport Central Bus Map dated 1968 showing the North East Section

Vehicle Details

RLH 1-20   Classified 1RLH1   Weymann L27/26R (26ft x 7ft 6in)
RLH 21-76   Classified 2RLH1/1   Weymann L27/26R (26ft x 7ft 6in)

Height 13ft 4in unladen

RLH 4 (KYY 504) at Uxbridge Station.
Photo Alan B.Cross

Reg.No.	Stock No.	Chassis No.	Weymann Body No.	L.T. Body No.	Del Date	Reg.No.	Stock No.	Chassis No.	Weymann Body No.	L.T. Body No.	Del Date
KYY 501	RLH 1	9612E 5034	M 4351	7099	5/50	MXX 221	RLH 21	9613E 6949	M 5524	8032	10/52
KYY 502	RLH 2	9612E 5025	M 4350	7100	5/50	MXX 222	RLH 22	9613E 6954	M 5525	8033	10/52
KYY 503	RLH 3	9612E 5030	M 4349	7101	5/50	MXX 223	RLH 23	9613E 6948	M 5526	8034	10/52
KYY 504	RLH 4	9612E 5026	M 4348	7102	5/50	MXX 224	RLH 24	9613E 6963	M 5527	8035	10/52
KYY 505	RLH 5	9612E 5029	M 4355	7103	6/50	MXX 225	RLH 25	9613E 6961	M 5528	8036	10/52
KYY 506	RLH 6	9612E 5033	M 4352	7104	6/50	MXX 226	RLH 26	9613E 6969	M 5529	8037	10/52
KYY 507	RLH 7	9612E 5032	M 4353	7105	6/50	MXX 227	RLH 27	9613E 6960	M 5531	8038	10/52
KYY 508	RLH 8	9612E 5027	M 4356	7106	6/50	MXX 228	RLH 28	9613E 6959	M 5532	8039	10/52
KYY 509	RLH 9	9612E 5028	M 4357	7107	6/50	MXX 229	RLH 29	9613E 6965	M 5533	8040	10/52
KYY 510	RLH 10	9612E 5031	M 4354	7108	6/50	MXX 230	RLH 30	9613E 6968	M 5536	8041	10/52
KYY 511	RLH 11	9612E 5039	M 4358	7109	6/50	MXX 231	RLH 31	9613E 6956	M 5535	8042	10/52
KYY 512	RLH 12	9612E 5035	M 4360	7110	6/50	MXX 232	RLH 32	9613E 6971	M 5534	8043	10/52
KYY 513	RLH 13	9612E 5036	M 4359	7111	6/50	MXX 233	RLH 33	9613E 6951	M 5537	8044	10/52
KYY 514	RLH 14	9612E 5042	M 4361	7112	6/50	MXX 234	RLH 34	9613E 6974	M 5530	8045	10/52
KYY 515	RLH 15	9612E 5038	M 4362	7113	6/50	MXX 235	RLH 35	9613E 6953	M 5538	8046	10/52
KYY 516	RLH 16	9612E 5037	M 4363	7114	6/50	MXX 236	RLH 36	9613E 6950	M 5540	8047	10/52
KYY 517	RLH 17	9612E 5040	M 4364	7115	6/50	MXX 237	RLH 37	9613E 6964	M 5539	8048	10/52
KYY 518	RLH 18	9612E 5044	M 4367	7116	7/50	MXX 238	RLH 38	9613E 6955	M 5544	8049	10/52
KYY 519	RLH 19	9612E 5043	M 4365	7117	7/50	MXX 239	RLH 39	9613E 6966	M 5545	8050	10/52
KYY 520	RLH 20	9612E 5041	M 4366	7118	7/50	MXX 240	RLH 40	9613E 6958	M 5542	8051	10/52

Vehicle Details Continued

RLH 1-20   Classified 1RLH1   Weymann L27/26R (26ft x 7ft 6in)
RLH 21-76   Classified 2RLH1/1 Weymann L27/26R (26ft x 7ft 6in)

Height 13ft 4in unladen

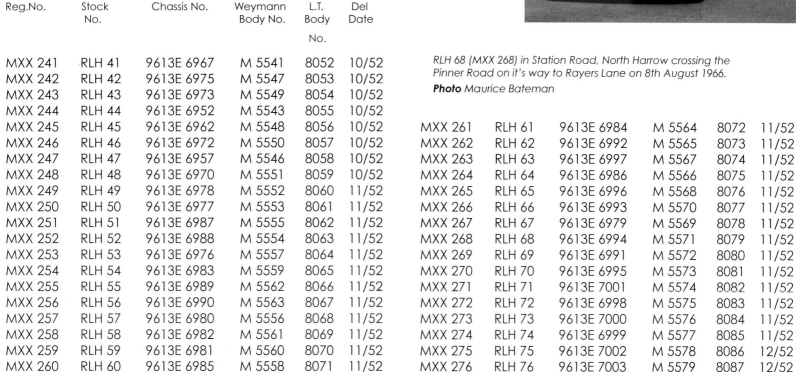

RLH 68 (MXX 268) in Station Road, North Harrow crossing the Pinner Road on it's way to Rayers Lane on 8th August 1966.
Photo *Maurice Bateman*

Reg.No.	Stock No.	Chassis No.	Weymann Body No.	L.T. Body No.	Del Date
MXX 241	RLH 41	9613E 6967	M 5541	8052	10/52
MXX 242	RLH 42	9613E 6975	M 5547	8053	10/52
MXX 243	RLH 43	9613E 6973	M 5549	8054	10/52
MXX 244	RLH 44	9613E 6952	M 5543	8055	10/52
MXX 245	RLH 45	9613E 6962	M 5548	8056	10/52
MXX 246	RLH 46	9613E 6972	M 5550	8057	10/52
MXX 247	RLH 47	9613E 6957	M 5546	8058	10/52
MXX 248	RLH 48	9613E 6970	M 5551	8059	10/52
MXX 249	RLH 49	9613E 6978	M 5552	8060	11/52
MXX 250	RLH 50	9613E 6977	M 5553	8061	11/52
MXX 251	RLH 51	9613E 6987	M 5555	8062	11/52
MXX 252	RLH 52	9613E 6988	M 5554	8063	11/52
MXX 253	RLH 53	9613E 6976	M 5557	8064	11/52
MXX 254	RLH 54	9613E 6983	M 5559	8065	11/52
MXX 255	RLH 55	9613E 6989	M 5562	8066	11/52
MXX 256	RLH 56	9613E 6990	M 5563	8067	11/52
MXX 257	RLH 57	9613E 6980	M 5556	8068	11/52
MXX 258	RLH 58	9613E 6982	M 5561	8069	11/52
MXX 259	RLH 59	9613E 6981	M 5560	8070	11/52
MXX 260	RLH 60	9613E 6985	M 5558	8071	11/52
MXX 261	RLH 61	9613E 6984	M 5564	8072	11/52
MXX 262	RLH 62	9613E 6992	M 5565	8073	11/52
MXX 263	RLH 63	9613E 6997	M 5567	8074	11/52
MXX 264	RLH 64	9613E 6986	M 5566	8075	11/52
MXX 265	RLH 65	9613E 6996	M 5568	8076	11/52
MXX 266	RLH 66	9613E 6993	M 5570	8077	11/52
MXX 267	RLH 67	9613E 6979	M 5569	8078	11/52
MXX 268	RLH 68	9613E 6994	M 5571	8079	11/52
MXX 269	RLH 69	9613E 6991	M 5572	8080	11/52
MXX 270	RLH 70	9613E 6995	M 5573	8081	11/52
MXX 271	RLH 71	9613E 7001	M 5574	8082	11/52
MXX 272	RLH 72	9613E 6998	M 5575	8083	11/52
MXX 273	RLH 73	9613E 7000	M 5576	8084	11/52
MXX 274	RLH 74	9613E 6999	M 5577	8085	11/52
MXX 275	RLH 75	9613E 7002	M 5578	8086	12/52
MXX 276	RLH 76	9613E 7003	M 5579	8087	12/52

Dates of Overhauls

When the RLHs were overhauled this was normally carried out at Chiswick Tram Depot and they retained their original bodies. Dates given are dates ex-works.

RLH 1	2/53	11/56	1/62	RLH 27	9/55	10/58	11/63	RLH 53	2/56	10/59	8/64
RLH 2	2/53	12/56	4/61	RLH 28	10/55	11/58	12/63	RLH 54	2/56	12/59	10/64
RLH 3	3/53	1/57	3/62	RLH 29	12/55	4/59	4/64	RLH 55	3/56	2/60	11/64
RLH 4	4/53	1/57	7/62	RLH 30	8/55	9/58	10/63	RLH 56	4/56	3/60	12/64
RLH 5	5/53	1/57	7/62	RLH 31	10/55	12/58	12/63	RLH 57	3/56	4/60	12/64
RLH 6	7/53	2/57	5/62	RLH 32	8/55	10/58	11/63	RLH 58	1/56	9/59	8/64
RLH 7	6/53	2/57	8/62	RLH 33	2/56	9/59	7/64	RLH 59	8/56	3/61	6/65
RLH 8	3/53	1/57	4/62	RLH 34	11/55	1/59	2/64	RLH 60	8/56	12/60	3/65
RLH 9	8/53	9/57	12/62	RLH 35	11/55	4/59	4/64	RLH 61	8/56	6/61	10/65
RLH 10	3/54	10/57	9/62	RLH 36	3/56	12/59	9/64	RLH 62	9/56	5/61	8/65
RLH 11	3/54	12/57	3/63	RLH 37	4/56	5/60		RLH 63	9/56	6/61	10/65
RLH 12	5/54	3/58	2/63	RLH 38	5/56	6/60		RLH 64	9/56	7/61	11/65
RLH 13	6/54	7/58	6/63	RLH 39	5/56	4/60		RLH 65	2/56	11/59	10/64
RLH 14	8/54	7/58	8/63	RLH 40	6/56	7/60		RLH 66	9/56	4/61	7/65
RLH 15	4/53	1/57	11/61	RLH 41	6/56	9/60		RLH 67	10/56	8/61	12/65
RLH 16	3/54	10/57	10/62	RLH 42	7/56	10/60		RLH 68	10/56	9/61	1/66
RLH 17	4/54	3/58	4/63	RLH 43	7/56	9/60		RLH 69	10/56	11/60	2/65
RLH 18	5/54	4/58	4/63	RLH 44	3/56	1/60	9/64	RLH 70	11/56	1/61	4/65
RLH 19	6/54	6/58	10/62	RLH 45	3/56	8/59	6/64	RLH 71	10/56	8/61	12/65
RLH 20	7/54	7/58	7/63	RLH 46	11/55	3/59	3/64	RLH 72	10/56	10/61	1/66
RLH 21	8/55	9/58	8/63	RLH 47	12/55	6/59	5/64	RLH 73	11/56	1/61	3/65
RLH 22	9/55	5/59	4/64	RLH 48	5/56	6/60		RLH 74	11/56	3/61	5/65
RLH 23	11/55	4/59	2/64	RLH 49	1/56	2/60	11/64	RLH 75	12/56	10/61	
RLH 24	8/55	9/58	10/63	RLH 50	1/56	7/59	6/64	RLH 76	12/56	5/62	
RLH 25	8/55	8/58	9/63	RLH 51	6/56	8/60					
RLH 26	10/55	1/59	1/64	RLH 52	7/56	10/60	1/65				

From Green to Red

RLH 1 to 52 were delivered in green livery followed by RLH 53 to 76 in red.

Eight of the RLHs received a repaint from Country Area green to Central Area red livery at the following dates:

RLH 1   November 1956

RLH 7   April 1959

RLH 9   September 1957

RLH 22   September 1955

RLH 23   November 1955

RLH 29   April 1959

RLH 49   April 1959

RLH 52   April 1959.

Most of these repaints were due to covering for Central Area RLH overhauls. RLH 62 was also off the road for months due to severe accident damage

RLH 1 (KYY 501) repainted into Central Area livery waits at Upminister Station.   **Photo** *Alan B.Cross*

A Day at work for the Addlestone Garage Staff

Country Area Vehicles at work from Addlestone Garage

Top Left - RLHs 31 (MXX 231) and 47 (MXX 247) at Guildford Bus Station.

Top Right - RLH 25 (MXX 225) travels along the newly opened link road between Weybridge and Addlestone.

Lower Left - RLH 33 (MXX 233) at Addlestone Garage.

Country Area 'Lowbridge'

RLH 1(KYY 501) passes under the lowbridge at Amersham Common on the 22nd October 1950.

Photo *The late John Gillham*

Central Area 'Lowbridge'
RLH 68 (MXX 268) passes under the 13' 9" lowbridge at Headstone Drive, Wealdstone on the main railway line in and out of London Euston Station. *Photo* Mike Hodges

Central Area vehicles at work

Above - RLH 17 (KYY 517) in the garage yard at Harrow Weald, alongside two Weymann RTs 3806 and 4558. Route 158 replaced the 114 in running to Rayners Lane in January 1966.

Left - RLH 65 (MXX 265) laying over at the Cranham stand of route 248 on the 12th May 1966.

Right - RLH 57 (MXX 257) in Headstone Drive, Wealdstone, on 20th April 1965 at the bus stop used as the crew change-over point for east bound buses.

Photos Maurice Bateman

Interior Views

RLH 48 (MXX 248) preserved and resident at the London Bus Museum, Cobham Hall, Brooklands, Weybridge, Surrey. **Photos** *Trevor Ryall*

RLH 64 (MXX 264) at Harrow Weald Garage

Chiswick LTE Engineering Drawings - RLH Elevations

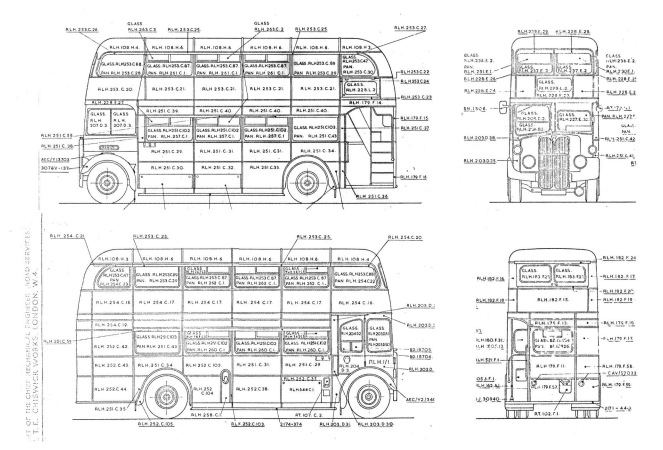

DISPOSALS

RLH 28 under tow in the California desert

DISPOSALS SUMMARY

Following their departure from London Transport the RLHs began a new lease of life, with many sold to overseas buyers.

Full details for all 76 vehicles are told in the next 45 pages together with a selection of photographs. A summary is shown for the 76 RLHs which is thought to be correct at July 2015.

Fully preserved and roadworthy (Total 10) :- RLH 14, 23, 24, 32, 41, 44, 45, 48, 50, 61

Under restoration or static exhibits (Total 11) :- RLH 4, 28, 29, 38, 39, 52, 53, 54, 62, 69, 71

Known to be in existence in recent years (Total 14) :- RLH 3, 7, 8, 15, 20, 21, 22, 25, 30, 34, 35, 60, 65, 70

Thought unlikely to be in existence now (Total 18) :- RLH 6, 9, 11, 13, 18, 19, 27, 31, 42, 43, 46, 49, 57, 59, 63, 68, 73, 74

Known to have been scrapped (Total 23) :- RLH 1, 2, 5, 10, 12, 16, 17, 26, 33, 36, 37, 40, 47, 51, 55, 56, 58, 64, 66, 67, 72, 75, 76

RLH 16 (KYY 516) Seen in August 1970 at Fort Wallington, near Fareham scrap yard with Provincial Guys in the background.

Photos *PM Photography*

RLH 1 **KYY 501**

| 22.12.1964 | Gliksten Services Ltd, Carpenters Road, Stratford, London E 15 |
| 17.11.1969 | O'Connor, 8 Lockwood Road, Ilford, Essex (Subsequently for scrap) |

RLH 2 **KYY 502**

10.02.1965	Passenger Vehicle Sales (London) Ltd, Upminster, Essex
03.02.1965	Exors of S Ledgard, Armley, Leeds, Yorkshire
15.10.1967	West Yorkshire RCC, Harrogate not used & stored at York Depot
12.1967	W North (P.V.) Ltd, Sherburn-in-Elmet, Yorkshire
01.1968	Passenger Vehicle Sales (London) Ltd, Upminster, Essex
04.1968	Nancy Taylor Career Courses, 35 Watchung Avenue, Plainfield, New Jersey 07060, USA
by 07.1969	Jimmy Byrne, Sea Girt Inn, State Highway 71, Sea Girt, NJ 08750, Derelict by 10.1987 & later scrapped

RLH 2 (KYY 502) in Rawden heading for Otley on 20th September 1967. **Photo** *Maurice Bateman*

RLH 2 (KYY 502) prepared for shipment to Nancy Taylor School in New Jersey USA. **Photo** *Maurice Bateman*

RLH 3 KYY 503

24.02.1965	Passenger Vehicle Sales (London) Ltd, Upminster, Essex
02.1965	Super Coaches (Upminster) Ltd, Upminster, Essex - fleet number RLH 531
	- carried Upminster & District fleet names for a time
01.1968	Passenger Vehicle Sales (London) Ltd, Upminster, Essex
	- repainted red livery retaining Super Coaches fleet number RLH 531
01.1968	Newport National Bank (contact G L Woodford Jnr), Newport Beach, California, USA
	- issued with tag ZXK 939
06.02.1970	Far West Services Inc, 1672 Reynolds Avenue, Santa Ana, California 92714 — still tag ZXK 939
05.06.1970	Harbor Island Hosts Inc, 1880 Harbor Island Drive, San Diego, Callifornia 92101 — still tag ZXK 939
18.01.1972	Walnut Properties, 5445 Sunset Boulevard, Suite 100, Beverley Hills, California 90210
by 02.1973	Aztec Bus Lines, 4437 Twain Avenue, San Diego, California 92120
09.1973	seen for sale on a vintage car lot in Encino, Los Angeles, California
by 03.1988	Sharon A Garaassino, -?-, California, later of -?-, New Mexico (bus in Santa Rosa, California)
by - 1990	seen in the Santa Rosa area

Reported owned by two women from Portland, Oregon who were taking the bus home when it broke down and it was taken to a yard at 2975 Dutton Meadow, Santa Rosa (which belongs to a Tom Vinci)
Bus had not been reclaimed and was still there in 05.1999

by 04.2005	Owner of RLH 3 now confirmed as Larry Wells, Rozwell, New Mexico — bus now in the care of Christopher Knott, who lived at 2705 Alton Lane, Santa Rosa but he has now moved and the bus was parked in a shed in the grounds of a house opposite. In 09.2009 bus was either in the care of or owned by Raymond Taylor, 2575 Alton Lane, Santa Rosa and parked in the field behind the house. Still there 06.2011
	No seats on either deck

RLH 4 KYY 504

11.12.1964	Passenger Vehicle Sales (London) Ltd, Upminster, Essex
16.12.1964	Exors of S Ledgard, Armley, Leeds, Yorkshire
15.10.1967	West Yorkshire RCC, Harrogate not used & stored at York Depot
04.1968	Passenger Vehicle Sales (London) Ltd, Upminster, Essex
08.1968	Ye Olde Kansas City Touring Association (S A Montague et el), 910 Pennsylvania, Kansas City, Missouri, USA
1969	Unknown owner, Oklahoma used to shuttle students between an apartment complex and University campus
1977	Seen at, and lettered for, Overton Square (shopping mall), Memphis, Tennessee
1989	Reported derelict at Fort Worth, Texas
c1993	Pat McDonough dba Natchez City Tours, 201 Somerset Drive, Natchez, Mississippi 39120
2002	Driven to River View RV Park, 100 River View Parkway, Vidalia, Louisiana 71373 (in effect 3 miles across the Mississippi River) and placed in open storage here
by 02.2008	Dean Hinrchsen, Mannheim, Germany, bus kept in Vidalia, Louisiana
11.05.2011	London Pub and Grill, South Sherwood Forest Boulevard, Baton Rouge, Louisiana
by 04.2012	In use as a static eye-catcher

RLH 5 KYY 505

27.03.1965	Seth Coaches, 41 Lismore Road, London NW5
c04.1969	R E Doyle (breaker), St Pancras Way, London NW 1
07.1969	Scrapped by Doyle

RLH 6 KYY 506

18.01.1965	Passenger Vehicle Sales (London) Ltd, Upminster, Essex
20.01.1965	Exors of S Ledgard, Armley, Leeds, Yorkshire
15.10.1967	West Yorkshire RCC, Harrogate, Yorkshire; not used & stored at York Depot
04.1968	Passenger Vehicle Sales (London) Ltd, Upminster, Essex
08.1968	Ye Olde Kansas City Touring Association Ltd, 910 Pennsylvania, Kansas City, Missouri, USA

RLH 6 Continued

by 01.1970	Samuel A Montague, Holiday Camps USA, Kansas City, Missouri
10.04.1970	Cheshire Inn & Lodge, 6300 Clayton-at-Skinner, St Louis, Missouri 63117 used to carry patrons with tag 464-002 in 01.1972
04.1991	seen in St Charles, Missouri owner unknown - tag OFX 381
by 09.1991	seen in St Louis advertising Deckers Restaurant tel 291-0330 — still with tag OFX 381
by 11.1994	Olympia Kebab Restaurant & Taverna (owner George Nicholas), 1543 McCausland Avenue, St Louis, Missouri - still owned 03.1999 and still driveable but under restoration
	No Further Reports

RLH 7 KYY 507

17.10.1967	Long Beach Public Transportation Co, 1330 Cherry Avenue, Long Beach, California, USA - shipped to Long Beach aboard the Queen Mary as deck cargo, and thus rounded Cape Horn! - tag E 518144. Used mainly for charters utilising the freeways
10.01.1975	Pioneer Theatres Inc, 2500 Redondo Beach Boulevard, Gardena, California 90247
c06.1983	in scrap yard at c.4000 Kettner Boulevard, San Diego, California
c1987	Gary Duncan dba Duncans Movie Magic (VHS movie rentals and I hour Photo), 108 SE 29th and 5937 SW 29th, Topeka, Kansas - still owned 08.1999 with Kansas Antique tag 11929
08.2002	Randy Wood, PO Box, 298 Centreville, Utah 84014 - for use in and around Salt Lake City
12.2008	Seen in storage in West Bountiful, 12.2008, ownership not confirmed but possibly still with Wood
by 04.2010	Seen in a yard on/near W 400 S (to east of US 1-15), seemingly in a reasonable condition. Maybe connected to a nearby antique shop.
02.2015	being advertised for sale, ownership unknown, advert still live 07.2015

RLH 8 KYY 508

29.01.1965	Passenger Vehicle Sales (London) Ltd, Upminster, Essex
03.02.1965	Exors of S Ledgard, Armley, Leeds, Yorkshire
15.10.1967	West Yorkshire RCC, Harrogate not used & stored at York depot
04.1968	Passenger Vehicle Sales (London) Ltd, Upminster, Essex
	- repainted into red livery and given fleet no RLH 51
06.1968	Piccadilly Inc, Mariemont Inn, 6880 Wooster Pike, Cincinatti, Ohio 45227, USA
1969	Boise Cascade Co, Ocean City, Maryland
	- seen at Cape May, New Jersey (by November 1969)
	Fitted with a Dodge V8 petrol engine and manual transmission
Unknown	The Chambers Restaurant Inc, Easton, MD 21601 and operated by London Bus of Talbot Inc
	(an associated business)
	Used in the film "Oh Heavenly Dog (Benje)" in 1980 as a London bus complete with LT white solid roundals
by 10.1989	Tom Troxell, Coopersburg, Pennsylvania
c1998	W J (Bill) Sobers, Koehler Road, Saylorsburg, PA 18353
	- in 2004 used by Cherry Valley Vineyards in connection with weddings held there, but not continued with the following year
	- still owned 03.2010, still displaying Cherry Valley Vineyards lettering

Left - RLH 8 (KYY 508) whilst operating for Samuel Ledgard on 19th September 1967. **Photo** Maurice Bateman

Right - RLH 8 (KYY 508) seen at Cape May, New Jersey in 1969 clearly displaying RLH51 fleet number. **Photo** M. Bateman Collection

RLH 9 **KYY 509**

08.07.1966	Leyland Motors Ltd, Berkley Square House Berkley Square. London WI — as agents
1966	Frank Sillers, -?- , Michigan, USA
	- Sillers based the bus in the Tampa - St Petersburg area of Florida and made it available for promotions, hires etc. Carried 'Double deck Tours of America' name on the lower side carried Michigan commercial tag 69806 - C in Florida 12.1966
by 02.1967	with Jim Hellinger (advertising etc), St Petersburg Beach, Florida, USA
	Not Traced Further

RLH 10 **KYY 510**

28.02.1966	Dagenham Motors Ltd, Sangley Road, Catford London SE6 — as agents for
02.1966	Elkes Biscuits Ltd, Dove Valley Bakeries, Cheadle Road, Uttoxeter, Staffs, for use as staff bus
c01.1971	Sold for scrap

Left - *RLH 12 (KYY 512) Elkes Biscuits first used as a staff bus at their Cardiff factory, where it was seen in May 1966.*

Photo *Maurice Bateman*

Right - *RLH 13 (KYY 513) in use with Trebor Mints as staff transport.*

Photo *Alan B.Cross*

RLH 11 KYY 511

23.05.1966   Massey Junior College, Henry Grady Square NW, Atlanta, Georgia 30303, USA
- unloaded from ship 'American Commander' in New York City 31.05.1966 and then driven to Atlanta
- operated in L T green livery on between the College and students dormitries
- tag 1284, named 'Piccadilly Peach'

by 09.1978   Joe Martin dba "Den of Antiquity", dealer in bric-a-brac, on State Highway 170 near Beaufort, South Carolina tag SC 6213. Mr Martin passed away in 1989 and his widow and the bus subsequently moved away.
Not traced further

RLH 12 KYY 512

28.02.1966   Dagenham Motors Ltd, Sangley Road, Catford London SE6 — as agents for

02.1966   Elkes Biscuits Ltd, Dove Valley Bakeries, Cheadle Road, Uttoxeter, Staffs, for use as staff bus based first at their Cardiff factory, later at Uttoxeter and later still at Burscough Bridge, Lancashire.

c12.1970   Sold at Bradshaws Motors, Lower Penwortham, Preston, Lancashire

10.1971   Barraclough (Breaker), Barnsley

RLH 13 KYY 513

01.01.1970   London Country Bus Services Ltd, Bell Street, Reigate, Surrey RH2 7LE

01.1971   Passenger Vehicle Sales (London) Ltd, Boars Tye Road, Silver End, Essex

03.1971   Trebor-Sharps Ltd, Woodford Green, Essex
- used as a staff bus to from the former Clarnico factory in Waterden Road, Stratford, E 15

11.1973   E H Brakell (dealer), 13 Palmer Avenue, Cheam, Surrey

14.12.1973   London Bus Preservation Group Ltd, Cobham Bus Museum, Redhill Road, Cobham, KT11 1EF - repainted red

12.1974   A.S.B 'uitzenbureau, 97 Nieuwre Parklaan, The Hague, The Netherlands
- used for promotions etc, still owned 06.1978, Not traced further

RLH 14 KYY 514

01.01.1970	London Country Bus Services Ltd, Bell Street, Reigate, Surrey RH2 7LE
01.1971	Passenger Vehicle Sales (London) Ltd, Boars Tye Road, Silver End, Essex
	- on Lesney Products contract from by 09.1971 to 09.1972, painted blue
09.10.1972	- painted red and used on British week events in Saltzburg, AUSTRIA
	- on loan to Peinelt Motors, Schleibheimer Strasse 395A, Munich, GERMANY (a film company)
	- returned to the UK
04.1973	Pennsylvania State University, University Park, State College, Pennsylvania 16801, USA
c1985	Wise Brothers, Spring Malls, Pennsylvania 16875
	- never used, just parked in a field of sheep!
c1990	Nittany Antique Machinery Association, Pennsylvania Cave Centre Hall, Pennsylvania 16828
	- normally used two weekends a year when the Association holds open days at its' showground, it provides shuttles between the car parks and the showground
	- still owned 09.2012, tag 31 EA (PA Antique Car series)

RLH 15 KYY 515

17.03.1965	Passenger Vehicle Sales (London) Ltd, Upminster, Essex
03.1965	Super Coaches (Upminster) Ltd, Upminster, Essex
04.1967	Passenger Vehicle Sales (London) Ltd, Upminster, Essex
	- repainted into red livery
05.1967	Newport National Bank (contact G L Woodford Jnr), Newport Beach, California, USA
	- being used to ferry passengers at Newport airport (reported in 1968)
by 03.1975	Tropicana Village, 55 North Broad Street, San Luis Obispo, California 93401
1977	British Double Decker Tours Inc, Vancouver, British Colombia, CANADA
1979	Marguerite Tours, Victoria, Vancouver Island, BC - Possibly not used
09.1979	Cunningham, Port Townsend, Washington, USA

RLH 15 Continued

06.1980	Thomas Kohr, Wenatchee, Washington
06.1982	John & Polly Dickenson and Bill & Diane Barkhimer, White Salmon, Washington
01.1990	Mike Hackett, Milwaukie, Oregon
11.1990	Jerry Barron, 7220 South West Shady Court, Portland, Oregan
	- retained as a classic vehicle and kept at the side of his house.
02.2002	Melvin J Peat, 947 Pine Street, Rogue River, Oregon 97537,
	- in use as a roadside coffee shop named Double Expresso Bus near Gold Hill - Medford by 09.2003;
	- still owned 10.2012 but stored in Peat's front garden although advertised for sale in 2011-12

RLH 16 KYY 516

28.02.1966	Dagenham Motors Ltd, Sangley Road, Catford London SE6 — as agents for
02.1966	Elkes Biscuits Ltd, Dove Valley Bakeries, Cheadle Road, Uttoxeter, Staffs, used as a staff bus
08.1970	Body only, partially scrapped at Fort Wallington Car Breakers, Fareham, Hants; chassis untraced
12.1970	K C Commercials Ltd, Belgrave Road, Portswood, Southampton, Hants

RLH 18 (KYY 518) seen during 1975 at the Trolley Square Shopping Centre, Salt Lake City, Utah.

RLH 17 KYY 517

06.09.1967   Elkes Biscuits Ltd, Dove Valley Bakeries, Cheadle Road, Uttoxeter, Staffs
                      - used as staff bus at their Burscough, Lancs, factory, Later fitted with platform doors
10.1971   Bradshaws Motors, Lower Penwortham, Preston, Lancashire
01.1972   Geoff Lister (dealer), Bolton
01.1972   Barraclough, Barnsley — broken at Lower Penwortham and remains taken to Barnsley by lorry

RLH 18 KYY 518

15.09.1967   M & M Charter Bus Lines (Associated Charter Bus Co), 9145 Evans Avenue, San Fransico, California, USA
by 07.1971   Salt Lake Transportation co, 346 West South Temple, Salt Lake City, Utah 84110
                      - painted red , with tag 263 424 and used on Gray Line Motor Tours work, still owned 05.1973
by 07.1975   Trolley Square (a shopping centre), 602 E 500 South, Salt Lake City, Utah 84403
                      - but still operated by Salt Lake Transportation Co with tag TT 7833
by 1983   Believed either owned by a company that hired canoes etc, or by an amusement park, at Saltair III
                      "Great Saltair", an entertainment venue just north of 1-80 17 miles west of Salt Lake City.
                      - whole area was extensively flooded by the Lake in 1983 and it remained so for several years, damaging the bus beyond repair
                      - bus seen derelict here ("at an amusement park by the Great Salt Lake") 04.1993
                      - gone from here by 11.1993, Not traced further

RLH 19 KYY 519

12.10.1966   Massey Junior College, Henry Grady Square NW, Atlanta, Georgia 30303, USA
                      - tag 1285, named 'Piccadilly Pete'
                      - still in use 05.1974
                      Not traced further

RLH 20 KYY 520

10.05.1968   R Allan Pommer, 898 Hyde Park Avenue, Hyde Park (Boston), Massachusetts 02136, USA —
for preservation COA to Maynard, MA 01754, and later to Bolton, MA 01740
- later kept at Clarke's Trading Post, 110 Daniel Webster Hwy, Lincoln, New Hampshire still there 10.2001
- parked behind a house on US Hwy 3 just north of Clarke's Trading Post 09.2006, with paint
work almost now down to bare metal. Still there 07.2015 but not used for nearly thirty years.

RLH 20 (KYY 520) seen at Clark's Trading Post New Hampshire during June 1978. Believed to remain unused for the past 30 or more years.

Photos A.Pommer

Left - RLH 21 (MXX 221) seen at Sheraton Hotel, Heathrow during May 1975.

Right - RT 3672 and RLH 21 seen in later life whilst owned by Steele Realty in the late 1990's.
Photo Bob Martin

RLH 21 MXX 221

01.01.1970	London Country Bus Services Ltd, Bell Street, Reigate, Surrey RH2 7LE
01.1971	Passenger Vehicle Sales (London) Ltd, Boars Tye Road, Silver End, Essex
03.1971	Trebor-Sharps Ltd, Woodford Green, Essex
	- used as a staff bus to from the former Clarnico factory in Waterden Road, Stratford, E 15
01.06.1973	Ensign Bus Co Ltd (dealer), 8 Wych Elm Road, Hornchurch, Essex
	- on Lesney contract from by 09.1973 to 10.1974
10.1974	London Bus Preservation Group Ltd, Cobham Bus Museum, Redhill Road, Cobham, KT11 IEF as dealers - repainted red and fitted with roof marker lights
03.1975	Omnibus Promotions Ltd, 39 Mitchell Street, London ECIV 30D
	- used for promotions and also as a spare bus on the Sheraton Hotel contract at Heathrow from 05 to 09.1975
11.1975	British Promotions Ltd, Suite 1210 United Virginia Bank Building, Norfolk, Virginia 23510, USA
by 02.1976	Buckingham Realty, Suite 101 814 South Westgate, Los Angeles, California 90049
by 09.1979	Unitrans (ASUCD) University of California, Davis, California, initially acquired for use on the freeways but was in the end never put into use
29.10.1981	Sold at auction by Dell Shuffield Auction Co, 712 Garden Highway, Yuba City California 95991
10.1981	Steele Realty, 8900 Grantline Road, Sheldon, South Sacremento, California without a power train —still there 05.1992 & 05.1999 (Location also given as being Elk Grove previously to 05.1999)
by 08.2000	Bud Wallace c/o Red Rock Winery & Brewery, 7326 E Highway 142, Merced, California 95344 bus still there 05.2011 although the Winery had closed- Wallace still owns Wallace Transport, on State Highway 140 at Planada, bus moved to Planada by 05.2012 and still owned 05.2014

RLH 22 MXX 222

15.11.1967	Russ Bramblett Leasing, 415 East Paces Ferry Road NE, Atlanta Georgia, USA
1969	Royal Coach Motor Hotel, Interstate-75 at Howell Mill Road, Atlanta, Georgia 30302
	later address recorded as being 1750 Commerce Drive, Atlanta, Georgia 30325
by 1991	Unknown owner and location, painted red/white band with lettering for 'Mid West Furniture Center' Phone no' 256-0800' & adverts for 'Coach & Horses Restaurant'
Unknown	Long Lines (The Telephone Company?), Okoboji, Iowa - said to be stored in Sargeant Bluff
by 01.2005	Unknown owner, Sioux City, Lowa
by 03.2006	Unknown owner, Drexel, Missouri, still carrying the 'Mid West Furniture' etc lettering

RLH 23 MXX 223

28.09.1967	David Pring, St Albans, Hertfordshire - for preservation
	- continued in preservation and later returned to PSV status for his Timebus Travel business, Still owned

RLH 24 MXX 224

01.01.1970	London Country Bus Services Ltd, Bull Street, Reigate, Surrey RH2 7LE
01.1971	Passenger Vehicle Sales (London) Ltd, Boars Tye Road, Silver End, Essex
03.1971	Trebor-Sharps Ltd, Woodford Green, Essex - used as staff bus to & from the former Clarnico factory in London, E15
03.1973	Passenger Vehicle Sales (London) Ltd, Boars Tye Road, Silver End, Essex
14.05.1973	British Leyland agents in Geneva, SWITZERLAND and used by a department store
by 08.1984	Shoppyland Schönbül (a hypermarket), Industriestrasse 10, 3122 Schönbühl (near Berne)
09.1986	Marco Ghidorzi t/a London Bus Ghidorzi AG, Wifenchauzweg 32, 4057 Basel
	- fully rebuilt and painted red, with PSV status, and used for promotions, weddings and charters registered BS1850 still owned 09.1994
09.2012	Seen near Frenkendorf, Switzerland 09.2012 — ownership not confirmed but still displaying London Bus contact details. NB London-Bus Ghidorzi AG in dissolution November 2012 + deleted from Business Register 23.01.2014

Above - RLH 23 (MXX 223) seen at Staines on the 30th July 1995 exactly 20 years after the withdrawal of the Country Area RLHs.
Photo Alan Conway

Right - RLH 25 (MXX 225) seen with Krewe of Kut-Ups.
Photo Bob Martin

RLH 25 MXX 225

01.01.1970	London Country Bus Services Ltd, Bell Street, Reigate, Surrey RH2 7 LE
01.1971	Passenger Vehicle Sales (London) Ltd, Boars Tye Road, Silver End, Essex
03.1971	Albert Verriest t/a Géné-Electra, Promotion Dept., 33-35 Rue de l'Orient, Brussels 4, BELGIUM
03.1973	Omnibus Promotions Ltd, 39 Mitchell Street, London ECIV 30D
	UK British Promotions Ltd, Suite 1210 United Virginia Bank Building, Norfolk, Virginia 23510, USA
	American Real Estate Corp, PO Box 5188, 985 Interstate 10N, Beaumont, Texas 77702 - tag U 9061 issued 1975
10.09.1976	Beaumont Convention & Visitor Bureau, PO Box 3150, Beaumont, Texas 77704
03.1983	- tag U 9061

RLH 25 MXX 225 Continued

by 05.1998   Mr Sligar Jnr, and parked outside Dippitys Hamburger Bar, Kountze
              bus ownership passed to Leslie Sligar, Lumberton, Texas 77657
              - bus eventually became a wreck which had sunk into the ground

c2001   Krewe of Kut-Ups (a group of friends), Port Arthur, Texas bus donated to them by Leslie Sligar for use in the Port
              Arthur Mardi Gras parade held every February
              - bus registered to Liz Holmes, Port Arthur but kept at the home of Kelly & Renee Taylor, in Port Althur Texas
              - bus transformed into a towable green, yellow & purple float minus all side & rear glass, but it was hoped to
              make it driveable again, Still had tag U 9061 in 05.2002
              - last reported in the Port Arthur Mardi Gras parade in February 2008, still as a non-runner.

RLH 26 MXX 226

01.01.1970   London Country Bus Services Ltd, Bell Street, Reigate, Surrey RH2 7LE
01.1971   Passenger Vehicle Sales (London) Ltd, Boars Tye Road, Silver End, Essex
02.11.1971   London Bus Preservation Group Ltd, Cobham Bus Museum, Redhill Road, Cobham, KTll IEF repainted into L T
              red livery prior to export to
01.1972   Bernice P Bishop Museum, PO Box 6037, Honolulu, Hawaii 9681B, USA - tag N 2151
              c1984 John Webber dba Kailu Wrecker, Honolulu for scrap

Left- RLHs 47, 36, 33 and 26 seen at the well known coaching 'Half Way House' stop on the A12 at Hatfield Peveral, Essex on 19th January 1972. Shipment was from Harwich Docks to Hawaii.

Photo Maurice Bateman

Right - RLH 26 (MXX 226) in Hawaii during January 1980.

RLH 27 MXX 227

05.09.1969	Massey Junior College, Henry Grady Square NW, Atlanta, Georgia 30303, USA

05.09.1969   Massey Junior College, Henry Grady Square NW, Atlanta, Georgia 30303, USA
- tag 1288.
01.1974   still owned
by 09.1978   Joe Martin "Den of Antiquity", a dealer in bric-a-brac, on State Highway 170 near Beaufort, South Carolina
- tag SC 6212. Mr Martin passed away in 1989 and his widow and the bus subsequently moved away.
Not traced further

RLH 28 MXX 228

15.09.1967   M & M Charter Bus Lines (Associated Charter Bus Co), 9145 Evans Avenue, San Fransico, California 94124 USA
NOTE. This bus carried UK plate KYY 517 on the radiator probably from when exported by London Transport
- tag X 17576 and with fleet no. 1001
26.02.1971   Pioneer Theatres Inc, 2500 Redondo Beach Boulevard, Gardena, California 90247 - used on a swapmeet
shuttle bus park and ride service
- Worked as a shuttle bus for customers at the Roadium swap meet
1975   Country Tire, 2317 Main Street, Ramona California 92065
- used as an eye-catcher outside this tyre depot
c1995   Bill Bowen, Bill Bowen Property Management Services, PO BOX 2115, Borrego Springs, California 92004 - located
in grounds of a house on Rango Way, Borrego Springs. Bowen intended
to restore the bus for his car collection but found it to be beyond restoration,
so it became a playroom for his children. Still owned 05.2005, then sold to a
local resident in Borrego Springs before being rescued by Grace Rickard.
02.2010   Mrs Grace Rickard, 737 San Pablo Road, Borrego Springs, California 92004

The complete story of RLH 28 since 2010 now follows

All photos by Grace Rickard

RLH 28 DESERT YARD ART

RLH 28 (MXX 228) - a story of rescue and restoration for a true London bus which had spent forty four years (1966 - 2010) in Southern California and was finally left abandoned, losing weight and depressed!!

Then in February 2010 it was all change for RLH 28 -.

During the 1990's RLH 28 was purchased by a couple who lived in the same village as Grace Rickard and her husband Jim; Borrego Springs, California, USA. Grace had a tender spot in her heart to own this bus and during January 2010 knowing it was parked almost derelict and available for possible purchase, she went with a friend to view up close, immediately deciding she wanted it as a static display on the lot beside her house.

It was then time to take her husband Jim along to view who was also moderately impressed and the deal was struck in February 2010. Next was to arrange the hiring of a pick-up truck with a strong rope, plus two persons who knew where the brakes were on the RLH for the four mile move to Grace's home and a welcoming party on arrival.

The body was found to be in substantially good condition and weeks of cleaning followed. Work commenced on fitting new windows where required, a completed new platform area plus many other minor areas of repair, finally being completed with a full exterior repaint to London Transport Red Central Area Livery.

As regards the mechanical side Grace states she is not interested in 'running a tour company' and just wanted the bus as a static display at her house and describes it as 'DESERT YARD ART'.

RLH 29 MXX 229

12.07.1972	Country Bus Preservation Group (sec C A Pearce) - for preservation and restored to LT country green livery
1987	D Pring, St Albans — for continued preservation
07.1988	BTS Ltd, Borehamwood, Herts (for PSV work & preservation)
02.1990	Marco Ghidorzi t/a London Bus, Wifenchauzweg 32, 4057 Basel, SWITZERLAND
	- partially dismantled for renovation and accreditation to psv status, not completed
05.2002	D Pring (Timebus Travel), St Albans, Herts, UK for preservation
	- towed back to the UK and is slowly being rebuilt

RLH 29 (MXX 229) in early stages of restoration close to Wimbledon Station.

RLH 30 (MXX 230) at Pipers Creek Nursery April 2012.

Photos - *Grace Rickard*

RLH 30 **MXX 230**

17.10.1967	Long Beach Public Transportation Co, 1330 Cherry Avenue, Long Beach, California 90813, USA
	- repainted red by London Transport prior to export
	- shipped to Long Beach aboard the Queen Mary as deck cargo, and thus rounded Cape Horn!
	- tag E 518143. Used mainly for charters utilising the freeways
22.03.1974	Norwalk Lions Club, Norwalk, California
by 10.1980	George T. Waterman dba 'Ye Old London Curiosity Shoppe', Kirkland, nr Seattle, Washington
	- relocated from Kirkland to 23730 Bothell Highway SE, Bothell, Washington 29.07.1985
05.06.1990	Rod Loveless dba Country Village, 23730 Bothell Highway SE, Bothell, Washington
	- bus still the centrepiece of a shopping village selling antiques
by 09.2009	Karen Whitfield, Bothell?, Washington - bus stored at Lynwood, still there 01.2010
by 02.2011	Alan Hensey dba Pipers Creek Nursery, 14061 Lake City Way NE, Seattle Washington 98125
	- livery is all red with ä silver roof For use as a static office
by 2013	Fred Klein, -?-, Camano Island, Washington

RLH 31 **MXX 231**

01.01.1970	London Country Bus Services Ltd, Bell Street, Reigate, Surrey RH2 /LE
1971	Passenger Vehicle Sales (London) Ltd, Boars Tye Road, Silver End, Essex
04.1971	Mariemont Inn, 6880 Wooster Pike, Cincinatti, Ohio 45227, USA
c03.1995	seen very tatty and vandalised parked in a field at junction Hamilton & Clermont, Anderson Township (East Cincinatti area) (together with ex Hants & Dorset Bristol Lodekka SRU 982)

RLH 32 (MXX 232) displays the Samuel Ledgard livery of blue and grey applied in September 2007 and was photographed at the London Bus Museum, Brooklands, Surrey during 2013. **Photo** Les Smith

RLH 32 MXX 232

01.01.1970	London Country Bus Services Ltd, Bell Street, Reigate, Surrey RH2 7LE
01.1971	Passenger Vehicle Sales (London) Ltd, Boars Tye Road, Silver End, Essex
	- used on Lesney contract, painted blue
01.06.1973	Ensign Bus Co Ltd (dealer), 8 Wych Elm Road, Hornchurch, Essex
	- still on Lesney contract until 10.1974
10.1974	London Bus Preservation Group Ltd, Cobham Bus Museum, Redhill Road, Cobham, KT11 IEF
10.1975	Geoff Harrington c/o 1 New Road, Ham, Richmond, Surrey
	- for conversion to a mobile caravan but not fully implemented
07.1976	London Bus Preservation Group Ltd, Cobham Bus Museum, Redhill Road, Cobham, KT11 IEF
21.11.1976	Peter Gascoine, Modelstone Bus Club - for preservation
	- restored to LT country green livery and later kept at North West Museum of Transport, St Helens
06.07.1997	D Pring, St Albans & R Proctor - for continued preservation
09.2007	- repainted in Samuel Ledgard blue & grey livery - still owned

RLH 33 MXX 233

01.01.1970	London Country Bus Services Ltd, Bell Street, Reigate, Surrey RH2 7LE
01.1971	Passenger Vehicle Sales (London) Ltd, Boars Tye Road, Silver End, Essex
01.1971	City Coach Lines (Upminster) Ltd, 168/170 Upminster Road, Upminster, Essex
06.1971	Blue Line Coaches, 168/170 Upminster Road, Upminster, Essex
10.1971	Passenger Vehicle Sales (London) Ltd, Boars Tye Road, Silver End, Essex
26.10.1971	London Bus Preservation Group Ltd, Cobham Bus Museum, Redhill Road, Cobham, KT11 IEF - repainted into LT red livery prior to export to
01.1972	Bernice P Bishop Museum, PO Box 6037, Honolulu, Hawaii 96818, USA
	- tag N 2146
c1984	John Webber dba Kailu Wrecker, Honolulu for scrap

RLH 34 MXX 234

01.01.1970	London Country Bus Services Ltd, Bell Street, Reigate, Surrey RH2 7LE
01.1971	Passenger Vehicle Sales (London) Ltd, Boars Tye Road, Silver End, Essex
04.1971	Southern California First National Bank, Box 1608, Newport Beach, California 92650, USA
11.1974	displayed at "Antiques Of the World", at 1957 Newport Boulevard, Costa Mesa, California
Unknown	William R Hamilton, 3010 Lafayette Avenue, Newport Beach, California
by 09.1979	Unitrans (ASUCD), University of California, Davis, California but not used
29.10.1981	Sold at auction by Dell Shuffield Auction Co, 712 Garden Highway, Yuba City California 95991
	Later seen in a tractor engineering works, Elk Grove, California and possibly still there 07.1997
06.2010	Still in red livery but in a very derelict state it was located in the Redding area of northern California and advertised for sale on Craiglist.
	Not traced further

RLH 35 MXX 235

01.01.1970	London Country Bus Services Ltd, Bell Street, Reigate, Surrey RH2 7LE
12.1970	16th Reigate Scout Group, Reigate, Surrey - repainted purple and used for transportation
03.1987	Marco Ghidorzi t/a London Bus, Wifenchauzweg 32, 4057 Basel, SWITZERLAND, never used - stored with Londag in Basel in 05.2002 but moved to another yard and seen stored 12.2004 Basel Not traced further

RLH 35 (MXX 235) stored in Basel, Switzerland and seen in the workshops of Marco Ghidorzi during 1988.

RLHs 37 and 48 (MXX 237 and 248) seen opposite the Hilton Base of Whippet Coaches in Huntingdonshire on 28th August 1967. They were normally used on school contracts rather than their bus services.
***Photo** Maurice Bateman*

RLH 36 MXX 236

01.01.1970	London Country Bus Services Ltd, Bell Street, Reigate, Surrey RH2 7LE
01.1971	Passenger Vehicle Sales (London) Ltd, Boars Tye Road, Silver End, Essex
01.1971	City Coach Lines (Upminster) Ltd, 168/170 Upminster Road, Upminster, Essex
06.1971	Blue Line Coaches, 168/170 Upminster Road, Upminster, Essex
10.1971	Passenger Vehicle Sales (London) Ltd, Boars Tye Road, Silver End, Essex
19.11.1971	London Bus Preservation Group Ltd, Cobham Bus Museum, Redhill Road, Cobham, K T 11 IEF
01.1972	Bernice P Bishop Museum, PO Box 6037, Honolulu, Hawaii 96818, USA
c1984	John Webber dba Kailu Wrecker, Honolulu for scrap

RLH 37 MXX 237

10.09.1965	Whippet Coaches, Hilton, Huntingdonshire —used as a school bus
c07.1969	Scrapped, remains to C E Street & Sons (breakers), Hilton, Huntingdonshire

RLH 38 MXX 238

10.09.1965	Whippet Coaches, Hilton, Huntingdonshire —used as a school bus
05.1968	F Cowley (dealers), Dunchurch, Warwickshire
07.1968	Passenger Vehicle Sales (London) Ltd, c/o ENOC Garage, Leigh Beck, Canvey Island, Essex
08.1968	Ye Olde Kansas City Touring Association (S A Montague et el), 910 Pennsylvania, Kansas City, Missouri, USA,
Unknown	S A Montague, 5508 Neosho Lane, Shawnee Mission, KS 66205
11.1973	British Promotions Ltd, Suite 1210 United Virginia Bank Building, Norfolk, Virginia 23510, USA
Unknown	Unknown owner, Wichita, Kansas
by 1985	Coloniel Heights Assembley Of God Church, 5200 S Broadway, Wichita, Kansas 67216
1986	Grace Baptist Church (contact Michael O'Donnell), 1414 West Pawnee Street , Wichita, Kansas 67213
	- had Kansas truck series tag EGU 634
	- was vandalised when parked beside the church so was moved to the pastor's father's house in south Wichita, just off Interstate 35.
03.2002	Randy Nix dba Gulf Coast Teleco, 26210B Equity Drive, Daphne, Alabama 36526
	- collected from Wichita 06.2004 & driven to Mobile, kept in building behind his house
	- tag VAM 725 (AL Vintage Vehicle series)
04.2013	- very slowly being renovated

RLH 38 (MXX 238)owned by Randy Nix of Alabana photographed at his premises whilst being restored during June 2013.

Photos - *Bob Martin*

Left - RLH 39 (MXX 239)two seperate views, seen firstly on the 30th August 1994 whilst used by McCulloch Realty in Lake Havasu City, Arizona.
Photo Chris East

Right - Later seen on 15th December 1995 out of service also close to Lake Havasu City.
Photo Brian Coney

RLH 39 **MXX 239**

17.01.1965	Associated Charter Bus Co, 5719 Sepulveda Boulevard, Van Nuys, California 91401 USA
Unknown	Sea World, 1720 South Shores Road, Mission Bay, San Diego California 92109
1971	Piccadiily Square, Fresno, California
Unknown	Foodmaker Inc, San Diego, California
06.04.1982	McCulloch Realty Corporation, 1690 McCulloch Boulevard, Lake Havasu City, Arizona 86403 - used as a static eye-catcher located at 2035 Palo Verde Blvd, Lake Havasu City (on the northern approach to Lake Havasu). Has tag MCCUL 3. Still owned 08.1996
by 09.2009	Steve Stocking dba Mudshark Restaurant, 210 Swanson Avenue, Lake Havasu City, Arizona 86403 - bus being completely renovated in their yard in Aviation Drive off Kiowa, Lake Havasu City 09.2009, but had not been completed as at 01.2014

RLH 40 **MXX 240**

12.08.1965	Richard D Lewis, Mobile Language Laboratories, 3 Campden Hill Towers, London WII - may have toured Scandinavia in 1965. From Motor Taxation records it was deduced that it had been abandoned in the Dartford, Kent area and was disposed of for scrap by the local council 09.1966

RLH 41 MXX 241

19.05.1965	Passenger Vehicle Sales (London) Ltd, Upminster Essex
05.1965	Super Coaches (Upminster) Ltd, Upminster, Essex
05.1967	Passenger Vehicle Sales (London) Ltd, Upminster, Essex
23.06.1967	Mariemont Inn, 6880 Wooster Pike, Cincinatti, Ohio 45227, USA
20.07.1970	The London Bus company, 7016 Euclid Avenue, Cleveland, Ohio 44103
by 02.1985	Firestone Tyre Depot, Wilmington Pike (south of East Dorothy Lane), Kettering, Ohio
	- tag 6519 H (an Ohio Historical plate)
02.1991	Sold to unknown US Airforce Captain, possibly for conversion into mobile restaurant and seen 12.1991 at Wright-Patterson Airforce Base, Fairborn, Ohio in as acquired condition
	Not traced in the intervening years
	Unknown owner, Marion, Lowa by 07.2009 when advertised for sale
07.2009	OK Bicycle Shop Restaurant, 661 Dauphin Street, Mobile, AL 36602 seen broken down on freeway at North Liberty, Iowa 28.07.2009 during collection!
	- This steak house & bar operates the bus on local charters. It is in excellent condition and largely in original condition. Livery Red with white waist band. Still on Ohio tag 6519 H
	- still owned 04.2013

RLH 42 MXX 242

17.03.1965	Harris Lebus Ltd, Finsbury Works, Ferry Lane, Tottenham, London N17
	- used as a mobile showroom painted blue/white
c06.1968	Nathan, London W 10 - as a mobile boutique
c12.1968	Sold, parked at A Weston & Sons, 1 Wood House Farm, Plough Lane, Wimbledon, London SW17
	Not further traced

RLH 43 **MXX 243**

07.09.1965	Harris Lebus Ltd, Finsbury Works, Ferry Lane, Tottenham, London N17
	- used as a mobile showroom painted blue/white
12.1968	Passenger Vehicle Sales (London) Ltd, Upminster, Essex and re-instated as a bus
03.1969	PVS Holdings Ltd — bus used on promotion work in Belgium, returned during 1970
1971	British Promotions Ltd, Suite 1013A Statler Office Building, Boston, MA 02116, USA
14.09.1971	Stew Jackson Enterprises, 3241 Alkire Court, Colorado — for his business
	Denver Burgular Alarms, 1955 Sherman Street, Denver, Colorado 80203
10.1972	- still owned but not traced further.

Left - *RLH 41 (MXX 241)seen in Alabana.*
Photo *Bob Martin*

Right - *RLH 43 (MXX 243)seen in February 1966 at the Harris Lebus Ltd factory in North London following conversion to mobile showroom for travelling across Europe.*
Photo *Maurice Bateman*

Rl H 44 MXX 244

01.01.1970	London Country Bus Services Ltd, Bell Street, Reigate, Surrey RH2 7LE
02.1971	- converted to Mobile Uniform Issuing store & numbered 581J in 04.1971
01.1983	D J Tippetts, Swindon, Wiltshire - for preservation
12.1990	David Pring, St Albans, Herts -for continued preservation

RLH 45 MXX 245

01.01.1970	London Country Bus Services Ltd, Bell Street, Reigate, Surrey RH2 7LE
01.1971	Passenger Vehicle Sales (London) Ltd, Boars Tye Road, Silver End, Essex
01.1971	City Coach Lines (Upminster) Ltd, 168/170 Upminster Road, Upminster, Essex
06.1971	Blue Line Coaches, 168/170 Upminster Road, Upminster, Essex

Top Left - RLH 44 (MXX 244) converted to Uniform Stores.

Photo London Country

Top Right - RLH 45 (MXX 245) at Robbie Murdock's garage on the outskirts of Christchurch, New Zealand in April 1999.

Photo Tony Hall

RLH 45 MXX 245 Continued

06.1971	Passenger Vehicle Sales (London) Ltd, Boars Tye Road, Silver End, Essex
11.1972	Bass International Ltd, London WI - as agents and exported to New Zealand
11.1972	Museum of Transport & Technology, Great North Road, Western Springs, Auckland, New Zealand
	- used for a free service at museum' sites, locally registered GJ 3835
by - 1989	Sold, believed to be with an owner in the Tauranga area
by 04.1994	R Murdock t/a Robbie's Fun Bus, Auckland, New Zealand
	- still owned 01.2015 when based at Ostend, Waiheke Island

RLH 46 MXX 246

01.01.1970	London Country Bus Services Ltd, Bell street, Reigate, Surrey RH2 7LE
01.1971	Passenger Vehicle Sales (London) Ltd, Boars Tye Road, Silver End, Essex
01.1971	City Coach Lines (Upminster) Ltd, 168/170 Upminster Road, Upminster, Essex
06.1971	Blue Line Coaches, 168/170 Upminster Road, Upminster, Essex
06.1973	Omnibus Promotions Ltd, 39 Mitchell Street, London ECIV 30D
08.1973	British Promotions Ltd, Suite 1210 United Virginia Bank Building, Norfolk, Virginia 23510, USA
09.1973	Tropicana Village, 55 North Broad Street, San Luis Obispo, California 93401
1977	British Double Decker Tours Inc, Vancouver, British Columbia, Canada
	- Not used and stored in the yard of Marguerite Tours, Victoria, Vancouver Island
by 09.1979	Sold
by 04.1980	Double Decker Hamburger Restaurant (Double Decker Family Restaurants of Canada Ltd), Willowbrook, Langley, British Columbia. Used as a static eye-catcher for the restaurant seen at Diamond Coach Lines yard at Highway 1 & 264th Street, Langley
01.1982	Later seen at Cloverdale, British Columbia
01.1984	Seen in Langley painted red/white and devoid of all advertising, owner not known said to be in the Fraser valley area but not traced further

RLH 48 (MXX 248) seen in Uxbridge on 12th September 1974 working on a promotion for a local radio station, London Broadcasting.

Photo Maurice Bateman

RLH 47 MXX 247

01.01.1970	London Country Bus Services Ltd, Bell Street, Reigate, Surrey RH2 7LE
01.1971	Passenger Vehicle Sales (London) Ltd, Boars Tye Road, Silver End, Essex
01.1971	City Coach Lines (Upminster) Ltd, 168/170 Upminster Road, Upminster, Essex
05.1971	Passenger Vehicle Sales (London) Ltd, Boars Tye Road, Silver End, Essex
19.11.1971	London Bus Preservation Group Ltd, Cobham Bus Museum, Redhill Road, Cobham, KT11 IEF
01.1972	Bernice P Bishop Museum, PO Box 6037, Honolulu, Hawaii 96818, USA
	- Withdrawn 11.1982 after termite infested tree crashed through the roof, then used for spares
	- Still owned 12.1983
c1984	John Webber dba Kailu Wrecker, Honolulu for scrap

RLH 48 MXX 248

10.09.1965	Whippet Coaches, Hilton, Huntingdonshire - used as a school bus
06.1974	London Bus Preservation Group Ltd, Cobham Bus Museum, Redhill Road, Cobham, KT11 1EF
by 09.1974	- leased to London Broadcasting Company as a promotion bus painted yellow until 01.1975
03.1975	James Walker & Sons Ltd, London WI - exported to their agents in Brussels, Belgium
23.12.1983	London Bus Preservation Group Ltd, Cobham Bus Museum, Redhill Road, Cobham, KT11 1EF
05.1984	Richard Proctor, Chertsey, Surrey - for preservation - restored to L T green livery - full restoration took five years to complete
04.2015	London Bus Museum, Cobham Hall, Brooklands Road, Weybridge, Surrey, KT13 0QS

RLH 49 MXX 249

05.1972	Gedol Italaxia, Lungarno a Besspucci 8, Firenze (Florence), ITALY
	- used by this oil-additive & lubrication business as a mobile demonstration unit with display equipment down stairs and a conference area on the upper deck
	- believed to still be owned 09.1973 Not traced further

RLH 50 MXX 250

01.01.1970	London Country Bus Services Ltd, Bell Street, Reigate, Surrey RH2 7LE
01.1971	Passenger Vehicle Sales (London) Ltd, Boars Tye Road, Silver End, Essex
01.1971	City Coach Lines (Upminster) Ltd, 168/170 Upminster Road, Upminster, Essex
06.1971	Blue Line Coaches, 168/170 Upminster Road, Upminster, Essex
06.1971	Passenger Vehicle Sales (London) Ltd, Boars Tye Road, Silver End, Essex
09.1971	Bass International Ltd, London WI — as agents and exported to New Zealand
09.1971	Museum of Transport & Technology, Great North Road, Western Springs, Auckland, New Zealand
	- used for a free service at museum' sites, locally registered FV 3835
12.1997	Bevan Welch, Kaukpakapa - bus thoroughly renovated and still owned 01.2015 when located in nearby Parakai. It has been offered for sale since 01.2012
	- advertised for sale on www.trademe.co.nz 02.2012 through to 05.2015, restoration not fully completed though bus located in a garden in nearby Parakai in 01.2015

RLH 51 MXX 251

29.03.1965	Office Cleaning Services Ltd, 1 Rufford Street, London NI
	- used as a staff bus based at their Longford, Middlesex depot serving Heathrow Airport
09.1968	Passenger Vehicle Sales (London) Ltd, Boars Tye Road, Silver End, Essex
09.1968	Poole Lane Autos (breaker), Highwood, Essex — and scrapped

RLH 52 MXX 252

22.04.1971	Quay Corporation, The Inn at the Quay, foot of Columbia Street, Vancouver, Washington 98660, USA
Unknown	The old Spaghetti factory, 152 South Monroe Street, Spokane, Washington 99201 - used internally in this restaurant with seats at tables on lower deck
06.2008	Mike Ferguson dba 1-90 Auctions, 11610 West White Road, Spokane Washington 98125
	- acquired minus engine & transmission, painted red and used as a static eye catcher on his property
	- still owned 09.2013

RLH 53 MXX 253

01.1972	Irving Perlitch dba Hill Country (a restaurant), 15060 Foothill Avenue, Morgan Hill, California, USA - bus was part of his Wagons to Wings Relic Collection
11.1993	Sold at auction when the Relic Collection closed down
11.1993	Don Vierstra, PO Box 219, 25500 Washington Street, Murrieta, California 92564
03.2007	Shawn McFadden & Melissa Walton, Ashland, Oregon
	- remained un-restored as such, offered for sale 02.2011
	- The RLH was held up at Baltimore Docks, Maryland, USA by legal issues for months and was finally shipped from Norfolk, Virginia in 03.2012, arriving at Liverpool 04.2012
04.2012	London Bus Museum, Cobham Hall, Brooklands Road, Weybridge, Surrey, KT13 0QS

RLH 54 MXX 254

20.03.1972	Promorama SA (M Maurice Cabo), 17 Rue des Firpiers Bloc 1, 1000 Brussels, Belgium
	- painted white with red roof and lower body skirt panels, fitted with an external sliding door to the platform and a large front bumper. Belgian/licence plates K.413.B In use as a rest room/store with a travelling children's amusement group
	- noted as such in St Idelsbald 08.1972 and in Bredene 08.1976
	- noted in De Paane 08.1980 still with the same Belgian plates (indicating that it was still with the same owner) but now painted red with white waist band
09.03.1981	Promobus International PVBA, 27-29 Dreve de l'Enfante, 1410 Waterloo, Belgium
	- roof fitted with a lift to raise its height when stationary. Front bumper removed. Now fitted with jack-knife platform doors. Belgian plates ANC 013
	- still in use 09.1984 when seen on a promotional bus service to an IKEA store in Brussels, Belgium
	- still owned 11.1996
by 06.2012	owner of London Gallery Europe (dealer in antique style English furniture), Chée de Vieurgat 305, 1015 Brussels
	- bus stored under cover, in poorish condition but receiving attention.
04.2015	unknown owner, in Germany

RLH 55 MXX 255

09.1972	Wombwell Diesel Co, Station Villas, Wombwell Yorkshire — and scrapped

RLH 56 MXX 256

05.12.1968	Passenger Vehicle Sales (London) Ltd, c/o ENOC Garage, Leigh Beck, Canvey Island, Essex
	- acquired minus roof after accident damage, stored with associated City Coach Lines (London) Ltd fleet in Clapton bus garage! later moved to PVS premises at Boars Tye Road, Silver End, Essex, used for spares
11.1970	scrapped by local breakers, Silver End, Essex

RLH 57 MXX 257

29.10.1971	Bruce Mulhearn Inc (Realtors), 16911 Bellflower Boulevard, Bellflower, Califorina 90706, USA
	Bus gone by 1992, business still functioning in 1996
	by 11.2004 Jerry Finch, PO Box 4714, 10859 Little Lake Road, Downey California 90241
05.2005	Nick Steel (young Nick) The Italian Fisherman, 10760 Riverside Drive, North Hollywood, California 91602
	- bus more or less complete externally and rubbed down to bare metal Internally completely gutted with no seats or staircase and half the upper deck floor gone. Probable use will be as a static eye-catcher
	- restaurant closed by 12.2008 and bus gone from site
	Not traced further

RLH 58 MXX 258

09.1972	Wombwell Diesel Co, Station Villas, Wombwell Yorkshire - and scrapped

RLH 59 MXX 259

05.09.1969	Massey Junior College, Henry Grady Square NW, Atlanta, Georgia 30303, USA
	- still owned 05.1974 and being used as a seat store

RLH 60 MXX 260

31.12.1969	Long Beach Public Transportation co, 1330 Cherry Avenue, Long Beach, California, tag 567314, used on charters
28.02.1975	British Promotions Ltd (West Coast office), Union Federal Plaza, 1700 Brookhurst, Fountain Valley, California
by 07.1975	London Line Realty, El Toro, California
by 09.1980	Blue Carpet Mobile Homes, 11810 Beach Boulevard, Stanton, California 90680
by 04.1985	Kobeys Swapmeet at the Sports Arena, Suite G 3770 Hancock Street, San Diego, California
c1994	Doug Green, -?- MEXICO - kept at Toy Storage, 1180 Industrial Boulevard, Chula Vista, California 91911, USA and used as a store. Still there 09.2009 with California, tag 029 MXB

RLH 61 MXX 261

21.04.1971	Quo Vardis Canada Club, 22 Great Windmill Street, London WI - and to. Quo Vardis Club Inc, 167 Church Street, Toronto 205, Ontario, CANADA, tag V77-952, later moved to 1606A Bloor Street West, Toronto 9, new tag 11-288
09.1973	D W Johnson, 11 Grenadier Road, Toronto 154, Ontario
by 09.1974	Travelway Tours Ltd, 120 Doncaster Avenue, Thornhill, Ontario - used in Ottawa in 1974 and in Kingston during the 1975 season on tour, returned to Thornhill depot by 03.1976
1976	Frontenac Coach Lines Ltd, Kingston , Ontario then Capital Coach Lines (Travelways), Ottawa, Ontario
1978	Travelways Maple Leaf Ltd, Ottawa, Ontario by late 1984 B Taylor, Strawberry Fields, Picton, Ontario
10.1986	Toronto Double Deck Services, Toronto, Ontario — registered BD9 424
1987	Furhman Auto Centre (dealer), Front Street, Toronto, Ontario — for sale
1990	Jack Innes, Oshawa, Ontario
c03.1994	Rob Garland, 119 Clover Ridge Drive East, Ajax, Ontario LIS IHI - bus kept at 8930 Baldwin Street, Myrtle and lower deck used to store garden plants - still owned 03.1999
05.2004	Ensign Bus Co, Juilette Way, Purfleet, Essex UK - restored to full PSV status on 22.07.2005 and is part of Ensign's heritage fleet - still owned 07.2015

RLH 61 (MXX 261) seen whilst in service in Toronto, Ontario, Canada with the rear view taken on the 28th March 1976 operating a shuttle service for the Sportsman Show in the Canadian National Exhibition Grounds.

Photos - *Paul Bateson*

Left - RLH 61 (MXX 261) looking tired and awaiting its future whilst with Rob Garland at Myrtle, Ontario on the 28th September 1995.

Photo - Bob Martin

Right - RLH 61 (MXX 261) Having returned to England and received a complete restoration is seen at Putney Common on 22nd July 2005.

RLH 62 MXX 262

31.12.1969	City of Columbus Transit Company, 10 West Long Street, Columbus, Ohio 43215, USA
	- given fleet number 1 and tag 149
01.1974	Change of entity to Central Ohio Transit Authority, 50 West Broad Street, Columbus OH43215
	- tag OE 128 issued 05.01.1974
08.1990	Smith Equipment & Truck Sales, Frank Road (exit 104 off 71 Hwy), Columbus, Ohio
12.2007	For sale on e-bay in quite good condition
03.2008	Jim Pullen, 407 Leppo Road, Westminster, Maryland 21158 for preservation
26.04.2008	Transported to Maryland for restoration to LT condition, kept on Jim Pullen's property - still owned 07.2015

RLH 63 MXX 263

29.07.1969	Diversfied Development Corp., 2011 Riverside Drive, Columbus, Ohio 43221, USA
	- for Arthur Treacher's Fish & Chips Inc, of the same address
by 08.1973	C F Egburt, Route 3, Lucasville, OH 45648
by 08.1977	Playpenn, 9900 Atlantic Boulevard, Diamond Beach, New Jersey 08750

RLH 64 MXX 264

09.1972	Wombwell Diesel Co, Station Villas, Wombwell Yorkshire - and scrapped

RLH 65 MXX 265

07.1971	Massey Junior College, Henry Grady Square NW, Atlanta, Georgia 30303, USA
16.05.1975	Highland Village (a shopping complex), just off 1-55 & just north of Jackson, Mississippi

- acquired direct from Massey Junior College
- mobile until circa 1998/99, with tag 943 in MI's Antique Car series
- during the Winter 2003/4 it was converted into a drive-by coffee bar called The Jumping Bean and stationed in the complex's car park.
- changed from The Jumping Bean to Java Werks (a coffee franchise)
- still in use 11.2011 but the Java Werks operation here is said to have closed permanently from 30.03.2012 and the bus was moved to another location within the complex. Still owned 01.2014

RLH 66 MXX 266

09.1972	Wombwell Diesel Co, Station Villas, Wombwell Yorkshire - and scrapped

RLH 67 MXX 267

09.1972	Wombwell Diesel Co, Station Villas, Wombwell Yorkshire - and scrapped

RLH 68 MXX 268

01.06.1971	City of Hampton, Department Of Commerce, City Hall, Hampton, Virginia 23369, USA
	by late 1974 Hampton City Transit Co
by 12.1976	Busch Gardens - 'The Old Country' theme park , Route 60, Williamsburgh, Virginia
c1977/78	bus disposed of, not traced further

RLH 69 MXX 269

01.1972	Irving Perlitch dba Hill Country (a restaurant), 15060 Foothill Avenue, Morgan Hill, California, USA
	- The bus was part of his Wagons to Wings Relic Collection
01.01.1993	Sold at auction when the Relic Collection closed down to.
	Don Vierstra, PO Box 219, 25500 Washington Street, Murrieta, California 92564
12.2006	Shawn McFadden & Melissa Walton, Ashland, Oregon (collected 03.2007)
07.2007	Bus restored and painted red with white roof, used in connection with their fashion business
02.2011	Offered for sale - Purchased by Peter Hobcraft, Bolebroke Castle, Hartfield, East Sussex, UK, for preservation
	- Finally shipped from Norfolk, Virginia in 03.2012, arriving at Liverpool 04.2012.
	- Due to delay in shipment and Peter Hobcraft sadly passing away, the bus passed to Roger Wright, London Bus Co, Northfleet, Kent

RLH 70 MXX 270

20.11.1969	E L Ansell, 1720 E 14 Street, Long Beach, California, USA
	- Ansell may well have been the owner of The Jolly Knight Restaurant (see below)
by 10.1980	Static eye-catcher outside "The Jolly Knight Restaurant", 8666 Garden Grove Boulevard, Garden Grove (greater Los Angeles), California 92644 - red with white roof livery
	Eye-catcher for Rose & Crown Pub, 831 S State Boulevard, San Clemente, California, Bus gone by/circa 1995
by 04.1997	Red Bus Rentals (Francesca Gallo), Suite 410 19528 Ventura Boulevard, Tarzana California 91356
	- tag RSE CRWN still carried in 2000; later tag changed to KAZ 846
	- bus used as an eye-catcher at Gary Realty, 21747 Erwin Street, Woodland Hills, California from by 04.1997 to c04.2001; in Topham 09.2002. Later on waste ground next to 156 Topanga Canyon Blvd (which is also California State Highway 27 in 04.2005. It had also been parked on California State Highway 1 (Pacific Coast Highway) at Malibu as an eye-catcher
	- bus parked at the back of storage yard in Uiley Canyon Road, Valencia Santa Clarita, by 09.2009
	- still owned 05.2015

RLH 71 MXX 271

01.1972	Irving Perlitch dba Hill Country (a restaurant), 15060 Foothill Avenue, Morgan Hill, California, USA
	The bus was part of his Wagons to Wings Relic Collection
11.1993	Sold at auction when the Relic Collection closed down to Don Vierstra, PO Box 219, 25500 Washington Street, Murrieta, California 92564
	- Vierstra intended to use the bus on local tours in connection with his real estate property business but the idea was dropped and it stood idle until disposed of
12.2006	Shawn McFadden & Melissa Walton, Ashland, Oregon (collected 03.2007)
	- bus restored 01.2010 and painted red with white roof, used in connection with their fashion business
02.201	Offered for sale
	Roger Wright, London Bus Co, Northfleet, Kent, UK
03.2012	For preservation. This was 1 of 3 RLHs (53, 69 & 71) which were held at Baltimore Docks, Maryland, USA by legal issues for months and were finally shipped from Norfolk, Virginia in 03.2012 arriving at Liverpool 04.2012

RLH 72 MXX 272

09.1972	Wombwell Diesel Co, Station Villas, Wombwell Yorkshire and scrapped

RLH 73 MXX 273

19.11.1970	Brauere Felschlosshen 45-47 Ludwigshafen RHN Oggersheim, Postfach 50, GERMANY
07.1975	seen at Saarbrucken University Campus promoting "Walsheim" with the lower deck in use as tasting rooms
c1988	F. Keller, Saarbrucken
	- in poor condition and disused/abandoned 05.1998
	Not traced further

Left - *RLH 71 (MXX 271) out of service in Murrieta, South California* **Photo** - *Dave Humphrey.*

Right - *RLH 73 (MXX 273) at the University Campus in Saarbrucken, West Germany. It is advertising the local brewery with the interior slightly converted to make a 'tasting room' on the lower deck. Photographed 1979.*

Photo - *Brian Gentle*

RLH 74 MXX 274

31.12.1969   Massey Junior College, Henry Grady Square NW, Atlanta, Georgia 30303, USA
              - still in use 05.1974
              Not traced further

RLH 75 MXX 275

08.07.1966   Leyland Motors Ltd, Berkeley Square House, Berkeley Square. London W1 - as agents
              unknown owner, seen at a brewery in Natick, MA 08.1966
              unknown owner, seen in Boston, MA, USA 09.1966 being used to promote Carlings beer
by 07.1984   derelict with Chicago Motor Coach Company, Chicago, Illinois
              - remains disposed of

RLH 76 MXX 276

27.06.1966	Dagenham Motors Ltd, Sangley Road, Catford London SE6 — as agents for
06.1966	Elkes Biscuits Ltd, Dove Valley Bakeries, Cheadle Road, Uttoxeter, Staffs
	- painted red/white and used as a staff bus at their Burscough Bridge, Lancs factory
	- still at Burscough 05.1971 and later transferred to their Uttoxeter factory 1972
	- withdrawn by Elkes 02.1973
by 04.1973	Barlows (breakers), Ashbourne Road, Spath, Uttoxeter, Staffs
	- dumped in yard and filled & almost totally buried under other scrap material
	- site clearance began eventually c2007 and the bus gradually reappeared
04.2008	- the body dismantled in the yard and skipped between 17th & 24th April 2008
04.2008	Chassis only to Reliance Bus Works, Newcastle-under-Lyme, Staffordshire
	- chassis was scrapped 05.2008

Photos - RLH 76 (MXX 276) shown at Barlows (breakers), firstly in 1975 and laterly during January 1992.

Anniversary Tours between 1971 - 2006

31.07.1980	10 year Commemorative Tour of the final Country Area routes using RLH 32 from Addlestone and Guildford Garages.
19.04.1981	10 year Commemorative Tour of the final Central Area route 178 using RLHs 23 and 29 from Dalston Garage
30.07.1995	25 year Anniversary of the last lowbridge service in Londons Country Area using RLHs 23 and 48
13.04.1996	25 year Anniversary of the last London lowbridge service route 178 using RLHs 23 and 48
13.10.2002	50 year Anniversary of the London Transport RLH bus using five preserved RLHs operating several former lowbridge routes. RLHs 23, 24, 32, 44 and 48
16.04.2006	Running Day to remember route 178 - RLHs 23, 48 and 61

RLH 48 (MXX 248) shown outside the former Weymanns Factory at Addlestone on 30th July 1995.

Photo - Alan Conway

The Midland General RLHs

Vehicle Details

421-430 Weymann L27/26R (26ft x 7ft 6in)

Height 13ft 4in unladen Chassis AEC Regent III

Reg.No.	Fleet No.	Chassis No.	Weymann Body No.	Del Date
ONU 630	421	9612E 4721	M 4341	3/50
ONU 631	422	9612E 4722	M 4346	4/50
ONU 632	423	9612E 4723	M 4342	4/50
ONU 633	424	9612E 4724	M 4340	3/50
ONU 634	425	9612E 4725	M 4338	3/50
ONU 635	426	9612E 4726	M 4347	4/50
ONU 636	427	9612E 4727	M 4343	3/50
ONU 637	428	9612E 4728	M 4344	3/50
ONU 638	429	9612E 4729	M 4339	3/50
ONU 639	430	9612E 4730	M 4345	4/50

Top - *ONU 631 shortly after delivery showing original destination box and the crest as the fleet name.*

Photo *Maurice Bateman Collection*

Lower - *Midland General 429 pictured here in Mansfield in May 1963 awaits a relief driver before continuing it's journey to Clay Cross. An array of Midland General vehicles are seen behind the Regent.*

Photo *Martin Liewellyn/Omnicolour*

Late in 1949 an order was placed by Midland General with Balfour Beatty for 30 lowbridge vehicles. The low height requirement was due to a railway bridge just south of Bestwood Village in Nottinghamshire which carried a branch line into Bestwood Colliery from the Nottingham and Worksop areas.
The order was for AEC Regent III's with the 9.6 litre engine to be fitted with lowbridge bodies by Weymann of Addlestone. It was realised that a requirement of ten vehicles would suffice with the remaining twenty on order being offered to London Transport. These formed the first twenty vehicles of the RLH batch of seventy six vehicles.

By the time these vehicles were delivered in 1950 Midland General had changed ownership and now came under the umbrella of the British Transport Commission eventually to be known as one of the Tilling Group. These would be the last new vehicles to be delivered for three years.

The first six vehicles were put straight to work at Mansfield (Sutton Road) garage for routes B8 and B9, followed soon after by the remainder of the batch. The batch spent most of their life at Mansfield Depot, only occasionally straying to Langley Mill which was generally for repairs.

Although the chassis and body shell were the same as the London Transport RLH batch, that's where the similarities really finished. Inwardly the side walls and staircase area were painted blue rather than brown, seat backs were blue vinyl rather than green and of the course Midland General applied their own moquette. Outwardly there a were number of differences upon delivery. The Midland General batch incorporated additional air vents on the roof, hinged access panels were fitted to the lower panels for inspection rather than removable panels which were fitted to the London vehicles. In addition there was a spy hole on the offside adjacent to the fuel tank from which you could read the fuel gauge. The front side lights were of a smaller type than fitted to the London vehicles with the offside being mounted on a bracket rather than fitting flush into the bodywork.

The Destination display consisted of a three piece at the front housing route number, via points and final destination, with the rear having a two piece display. There was no destination display above the rear platform. The London RLH's of course had no rear destination blind but did have a destination blind above the rear platform.

Midland General made their own changes to the vehicles, probably the most notable was the repositioning of the front number plate traditionally fitted under the radiator, they were moved to the offside under the drivers' windscreen. As late as the early 60's indicator flashers were fitted a little distance behind the cab just above lower deck window level. Some other minor alterations were made to the rear view mirror design and to the front destination glasses which were re-glazed in rubber.

As mentioned above these vehicles were primarily purchased for the B8 and B9 services which ran from Mansfield to Nottingham via Blidworth and Hucknall, the latter being an infrequent service and eventually discontinued.

They were also put to work on other routes which did not require lowbridge vehicles as follows.

C3 Mansfield – Clay Cross   D1 Mansfield – Chesterfield
D4 Ripley – Chesterfield   D5 Sutton – Chesterfield
D6 Alfreton – Clay Cross

This batch of AEC's did not last as long as their counterparts in London with 430 being taken out of service prematurely in 1966 with the remainder of the batch being withdrawn in 1968. Amazingly like their counterparts in London a number of the Midland General batch have survived as follows.

Top Left - Midland General 426 although showing ultimate destination "Matlock" has performed service B7, from Ripley to Mansfield where it shares the Depot with cell mate 427. A Midland General MW can also be seen in the picture.

Photo *Nigel Hall*

Top Right - Former Midland general ONU 638 repainted red and seen in Euston, London en route for the docks being exported to the USA by PVS (London) in October 1968.

Photo *Maurice Bateman*

Disposals

421 **ONU 630**

07.1968	Passenger Vehicle Sales (London) Ltd, Canvey Island, Essex, repainted red
10.1968	F W Schermerhorn dba Colonial Motors, 40th & Market Street, Wilmington, Delaware 19802, USA
	Not traced further

422 **ONU 631**

07.1968	Passenger Vehicle Sales (London) Ltd, Canvey Island, Essex, repainted red and given fleet no. 'RLH 90'
1969	Robert Thomas dba British Promotions, Statler Office Building, Boston, MA 02116, USA
	- used for promotions and charters etc, then to unknown owner in Michigan
	when acquired by Chicago Motor Coach Company it carried lettering for 'Roller Skate Rental' , also '93 Q FM' and Majic Bus'
07.1984	Chicago Motor Coach Company, Chicago, Illinois
	- converted to open top 08.1984, numbered 509 and in use on sightseeing tours of Chicago 09.1984
	- probably withdrawn by 06.1987 and still parked in Chicago Motor Coach Company's 'graveyard' 08.1992

423 ONU 632

07.1968	Passenger Vehicle Sales (London) Ltd, Canvey Island, Essex, repainted red and given fleet no. 'RLH 78'
12.1968	Golan Import Co Inc, Van Nuys, California, USA
	- seen in a signpainters yard in Glendale, California 05.1969
	IJsed in the film Rainbow Edge made in summer 1970, ownership unknown
by 07.1975	Pioneer Theatres Inc, 2500 Redondo Beach Boulevard, Gardena, California 90247
	- lettered "H M B Interlandia Roadium Swap Meet" and used on a car park shuttle to the swap meet
by 11.1990	Seen 23.11.1990 with the roof removed above the windows parked ar Gardena dog track the day after the track has closed. Not traced further

424 ONU 633

07.1968	Passenger Vehicle Sales (London) Ltd, Canvey Island, Essex, repainted red and given fleet no. 'RLH 79'
05.1969	Piccadilly Inc, Mariemont Inn, 6880 Wooster Pike, Cincinatti, Ohio 45227, USA
by 04.1970	Jim Hellinger Corporation, 2646 Central Avenue, St Petersburg Beach, Florida. Not traced further

425 ONU 634

1968	Withdrawn by Midland General Omnibus Company after accident
12.1968	Scrapped by this date

426 ONU 635

07.1968	Passenger Vehicle Sales (London) Ltd, Canvey Island, Essex, repainted red
11.1968	Belk-Simpson Stores, Greenville, South Carolina, USA. Not traced further

427 ONU 636

07.1968	Passenger Vehicle Sales (London) Ltd, Canvey Island, Essex, repainted red
10.1968	Columbus Business University, Columbus, Ohio, USA
	- out of use with mechanical defects 1971, still owned 10.1972. Then no trace until 1989.

427 ONU 636 Continued

1989	Pat Donaldson, 1125 West 77th Street, Kansas City, Missouri

1989   Pat Donaldson, 1125 West 77th Street, Kansas City, Missouri
         - seen as 'Marsh's Suncrush' in Westport, Kansas City 29.8.2009
         - still owned in good condition with 'General' fleet name 11.2010

428 ONU 637

07.1968   Passenger Vehicle Sales (London) Ltd, Canvey Island, Essex
            - Midland General Omnibus Company front destination boxes removed and replaced with a large single
            name glass- Also fitted with Overton air-operated platform doors, repainted red and given fleet no 'RLH 77'
11.1968   Baltimore Business Institute, 10 West Chase Street, Baltimore, Maryland, USA
            - used for students transportation & projects
by 08.1969 Bill Gibbs, Ocean City, MD. Not traced further

429 ONU 638

07.1968   Passenger Vehicle Sales (London) Ltd, Canvey Island, Essex, repainted red
10.1968   Newport National Bank, 1957 Newport Boulevard, Costa Mesa, California, USA
            may have been with an enterprise called London Company in Scottsdale, Arizona
            -this may have been a travelling theatre company
by 09.1985 Argon Oil, Redlands, California
            - painted black & red, and still with London Company lettering on the upper side panels
            - still owned 09.2002
by 09.2007 Said to have been in a scrap yard near Davis, California and recovered from there 09.2007 and taken to the
            San Francisco Bay area, restoration said to be in progress 05.2008

430 ONU 639

1966   Withdrawn
            Disposal not recorded ?

The RLH Model

There are many models produced of London Buses especially in 1/76 th scale. Anbrico, a well known model kit company was the first to produce a model kit for the RLH and when constructed gave a finish as shown below.

Exclusive First Edition

Anbrico

Exclusive First Editions (EFE) followed with a series of completed models in liveries of London Transport Red Central Area, Green Country Area then followed a model in the Samuel Ledgard blue and grey and Midland General blue and cream liveries.